MW01493820

Cracking
the
Code
to
Profit

The Blueprint for
Building a Real Business in
the Lawn Care and Landscaping Industry

Ryan J. Sciamanna

authorHOUSE®

AuthorHouse™
1663 Liberty Drive
Bloomington, IN 47403
www.authorhouse.com
Phone: 1 (800) 839-8640

Published by AuthorHouse 01/23/2018

ISBN: 978-1-5462-2518-8 (sc)
ISBN: 978-1-5462-2516-4 (hc)
ISBN: 978-1-5462-2517-1 (e)

Library of Congress Control Number: 2018900686

Print information available on the last page.

Any people depicted in stock imagery provided by Thinkstock are models, and such images are being used for illustrative purposes only. Certain stock imagery © Thinkstock.

This book is printed on acid-free paper.

DEDICATION

This book is dedicated to my daughter Michaeyla. I love you so much and cannot wait to see your life unfold before my eyes.

EPIGRAPH

"Keep Making Money!"

CONTENTS

PREFACE

I am truly honored that you are reading my book. Before you begin I wanted to let you know that all references made in this book are included at the end of the book and are also on our website at LawnCrack.com/book-resources, so you don't have to stop to note these as you read. I also must add the disclaimer that this book contains my best advice from my experience starting, running, and growing my lawn care and landscaping company. It should not be misconstrued as legal or financial advice in any way, shape, or form.

I hope you get everything you were looking for from this book and more. Thank you so much for reading it. I would love to hear what you think about it once you finish. Where to find me is also in the resources with all the links and other resources at the end of the book. I also have included action steps at the end of each chapter. Learning anything does very little for you unless you apply that knowledge. I wish you the very best in life and business.

INTRODUCTION

When I was ready to start my lawn care business, I asked my current boss at a local lawn care and landscaping company if it was okay if I began mowing lawns after I got off work. He said, and I quote, "There is enough grass for us all to cut." That was all I needed to hear! But, he continued, "If I could give you one piece of advice, don't do it." I was younger, 24 years old at the time, and thoroughly confused by his last statement. Long story short I didn't take his advice on not starting a lawn care business, but now I fully understand why he said it. I will come back to this statement at the end of the book.

Here is my advice to anyone considering starting their own company. Be prepared to work, a lot. I cannot stress this enough. Owning a business is not for everyone, especially a lawn care or landscaping business. There are a lot of moving parts. Whatever you think it will take, multiply that by 10. This is called The 10x Rule, which is also the title of an excellent book by Grant Cardone that I highly recommend. For you to compete and break into the market, you are going to have to work harder than you expect.

Personally, when I was starting my lawn care and landscaping business, I looked at it like I was training for a sport. If you are planning to make a decent living, be forewarned, this line of work is very physically demanding. That is one of the main reasons I spent so much time in the gym. I had to make sure I could physically handle the huge amount of physical labor and fast pace required each day. I continue to work out daily because I enjoy it, and truly feel like it plays a significant role in my ongoing success in business and life. Not to say that you can't be successful in this industry if you are not it great shape, but it certainly will help and make it much more enjoyable.

Lawn care and landscaping is a versatile business to start, in that you can start off part time making a little extra money, or grow it into a real, full-time business making a good living for yourself, eventually offering employment opportunities to others. It is up to you and what you want your lawn care business to do for you. This is the first important decision you need to make when starting your business.

My lawn care business went through all three of these phases, and I had success in each. I, unlike my previous boss, would recommend anyone who has a desire to start a lawn care company to do so. It is very satisfying and can provide you with more income than you could generate at most jobs, especially without requiring a college degree. With that said, it is also going to be more work, both in the field and in the office. So, before you begin, please honestly evaluate yourself to make sure you are ready to handle the bumps in the road because there will be bumps. If you are up to it, I congratulate you and wish you the best. You can make this happen.

Before we get too far along, I want to get a couple of things out in the open. Cracking the Code to Profit is a book packed with real-world advice gained from experience on how to grow your lawn care business into a money-making machine. I started my business with no business management experience what so ever. I did know how to perform the technical aspects of the business from working for other companies. I am a former drug addict, I have had numerous run ins with the law, and started my business with no money. I only tell you this to let you know if I can do it, so can you.

The reason my lawn care business became so successful is because I continued to educate myself on how to properly run a business, market, deal with people, and most importantly, how to think. Self-education is where I feel a lot of business owners fail and is ultimately why they do not succeed. As I said, this is a book on how to grow your lawn care business, but I do feel it necessary to include some practical general advice before we get started although this is not a self-help book.

When you go into business for yourself, you are going to lose the boss over your shoulder and the overall structure most jobs provide. What this means is you are going to have to hold yourself accountable and develop structure in your business. You need to be a self-motivated person. The first several years of my business I woke each morning at 5:00 AM and was working by 5:15 AM. I couldn't wait to get the next day started. I lost this drive my 6th year in business, and that is what lead me to change my course in life. I still love the lawn and landscape industry and am once again up at 5:00 AM ready to tackle the tasks of the day. My new passion is helping others achieve their goals in life, and there is no one else I would rather start with than you, and other lawn care and landscape business owners.

Your mind set is going to play a huge role in your success. By this, I mean the thoughts that you allow to dominate your mind, which will eventually manifest into your actions. You may call this your attitude. You will need to keep a positive state of mind. Henry Ford said, "Whether you think you can, or think you can't, you're right." This could not be truer. Ford also said, "Thinking is the hardest work there is, which is probably the reason why so few engage in it." It is very easy to get wrapped up in the day to day of operating your business and forget to think about how to improve.

I have found a great way to keep a positive attitude is to have a mentor or several mentors. In business, this could also be referred to as a business coach. If you think you can become successful without the help of others, you are wrong. Ask any successful person you know if they had a mentor. I guarantee they will say they did. The fact of the matter is, you don't even have to speak with your mentor. Your mentors can be authors of books you have read. Many of my mentors are well-known authors. Although I have never met these people, they have positively impacted my life, and I doubt I would be where I am without them. Another example that proves this point is professional athletes. These people are the very best in the world at what they do, and still, each and every one has a coach.

You will have to stay focused! If you truly believe in your mind that you will succeed in your business, you will have the wherewithal to push through the setbacks. Unsuccessful people do what they want to do. Successful people do what needs to be done, whether they want to do the task at hand or not. It is very important to understand the significance of those last two statements. If you are not willing to do what it takes to succeed, very simply, you will not.

You will have to make sacrifices. I will share a couple of the major sacrifices I made when starting my business. The first, and biggest sacrifice, was missing out on the early years of my daughter's life. She was born over the winter before my third year in business began. I still made it to all the major events, but I did not get to spend any real quality time with her as I would have liked for the first four years of her life. It is honestly still a little painful to think about as I cannot get those precious years back, but fast forward to today, and I have the free time and enough money to spend as much time with her as I possibly can. That is a great feeling.

The next big sacrifice I made was in the relationships with my friends. I had made up my mind that I was going to succeed and nothing was going to stop me. My friends did not have the same ambitions as I did and this lead us to grow apart. I spent all my waking hours learning how to become a better business person and building the foundation for a better tomorrow. They were content working regular jobs and just getting by in life. There is nothing wrong them, and I still enjoy their company when we occasionally get together. Some of my friends are doing very well and have moved away from home to pursue their professional careers. While some others are just now realizing the potential they have and are beginning to act on it.

The last sacrifice I will mention is my passion for sports. I was born in Cincinnati and grew up across the river in Kentucky. I was, and still am, a huge Reds fan. The only difference now is I can't name half the players on the team and don't have a clue what their record is. I also like to say if I hadn't snapped the ligament in my throwing arm and had Tommy John surgery my sophomore year of high year, I would be playing for the Reds right now. I used to watch almost every televised game. The bottom line here is, the time I spent watching the Reds was not doing anything for my family or me. I had to make a decision, and I decided my financial future was more important than the entertainment I would receive from watching them play. I know a lot of successful people who are big sports fans, but I know more who are not.

Maybe you have heard of Pareto's principle, which is often referred to as the 80/20 principle. This principle states that 80% of your results will come from 20% of your actions. It holds true in so many aspects of life. I now 80/20 everything in my life and strongly suggest you do the same. I have never heard anyone else combine the 80/20 rule with another saying, "If you say yes to something, you say no to everything else," but I am going to now. If you continue to say yes to the 80% of things on your to do list that are the easy, minimal impact tasks, you are effectively saying no to the 20% of the tasks that will yield 80% of your results. Your results will reflect this poor decision. Instead of letting the 80% consume all of your time because it will try, develop the willpower to knock the 20% out as early in the day as possible. As you add employees, delegate the 80% to them as much as possible. In the meantime, return that important email first thing in the morning, call your customer back to resolve whatever issue they have with your service, and reach out to the clients you wish you had. Not only will this increase your productivity immensely, but you will feel a great sense of pride knowing you did what had to be done. That positive energy will stay with you throughout the day, and you will feel yourself getting closer to obtaining your goals.

So, that is it for my little self-help rant that I felt had to be included in this book for you to get the most out of it. The best book you can read on this subject is Think and Grow Rich by Napoleon Hill. I have only read the book three times, but I met someone who has been reading it for 22 years at a networking meeting. His company is Maximizing Results, and I signed up for his webinar series where he breaks down each chapter of the book. It honestly changed my life, and I am confident it would do the same for you. If you want more information on that, check out http://www.MaximizingResultsLLC.com.

First things first, determine the goals of your business. What do you want your business to do for you? What are your long-term goals? Once you know this you can begin. You need to define success before you will be able to achieve it. Without clarity, you can only have confusion. Get a clear mental picture of what you want to achieve in your business and what that will look like. See your trucks, equipment, and employees. Also, see how you will be better able to support your family, what your home will look like in the future, what kind of cars will be in your driveway, and where will you be vacationing. This is what will keep you motivated to keep going. But please understand, if you don't know where you are going, how will you ever get there or even know if you got there? Don't skip over this step!

Introduction - Action Steps

1.– Take as long as you need to get a clear image of what your business will look like 3-5 years down the road. This image can change overtime, and probably should and will change, but it is still very important to 'see' it in your head.

2.– Do the same thing for your personal life as you grow your business. Business and life are very similar. You need to remain in a healthy state in each or you risk compromising the other.

3.– Consider purchasing Think and Grow Rich and joining the Maximizing Results webinar on the book. The principles to success in life are in the book and the webinar will speed up your comprehension of the principles so you can more quickly implement them into your life and business.

4.– If you don't already have an Audible account you can get your first 2 books for free by using our special link. Audible is Amazon's audio book platform if you did not know. The first 2 audio books I recommend for anyone starting a business are The E-Myth Revisited and How to Win Friends and Influence People. Think and Grow Rich is a book you should physically read, highlight, and reference daily.

CHAPTER 1

The Potential of a Lawn Care Business

Here is the reason I started my business. When I began working in lawn care and landscaping, I was on a 2-man crew, just the aforementioned boss' nephew and me. I asked him questions all day long until he inevitably said, "Ok, no more questions today." One day, before I reached my daily quota, I asked, "How do you guys get paid for doing these jobs?" He said, "We give the customers a quote for the work they would like us to perform, and if accepted, they pay us that amount each time we provide that service." My mind was blown because I was used to getting $9-$10 an hour as a cook or a helper before I started working there. So, I was like, "Are you telling me that it doesn't matter if it takes us 10 minutes or 2 hours to cut this place, they are going to pay the same amount?" He confirmed that is how it works. I was thinking to myself, 'You have got to be kidding me! I am a beast at this and fly through these jobs while still getting everything done perfectly. I could clean up if I had my own business.' And that was the moment it all clicked for me.

Although I don't know your situation, my goal for this book is to benefit as many people as possible. If you already have experience running a business, you may not need some of the information in this book. However, every bit of information in this book is tried and true, so you may find something that you had not considered before. Or you may find something that I overlooked! In either case, please feel free to contact me to discuss any topic in this book, or not in this book. You reach me by going to LawnCrack.com or connecting with me on any of the social platforms @LawnCrack.

As mentioned earlier, the most important thing that you need to define is your goal, or goals. It is certainly okay to have more than one goal at a time. Your goals are critical as you are getting started. Specifically, you need to determine your financial goals. Do you only want to get enough work to provide for yourself? For yourself and your family members and friends? Do you want multiple crews? Or do you want multiple locations in several states? Any of these scenarios are possible. Knowing what you are aiming for will guide you as you make decisions as your business grows.

Although I am not a hardcore business plan guy, I did write a business plan before starting my business. I would highly encourage you to do the same. If you are already in business, it is not too late, you can write yours now. A business plan is a living document, meaning you should come back and add to it over time as circumstances change and you strive to reach bigger goals. Your business plan will reflect your goals. Goals that are written down get achieved at exponentially higher rates than goals that only remain as thoughts. Go to SBA. gov and use their business plan builder. It will walk you through the process and make it very easy to do. Writing your business plan down is going to force you to consider many things you probably would not have otherwise thought. It is also the only way you will be able to come back to it and reference it. An important part of the business plan process is your mission statement. Your mission statement should be a paragraph that is laser focused on the purpose and intent of your business and should let people know why they should do business with your company.

One thing I wish I would have done earlier was financial forecasting. I know…it sounds intimidating, but it is not really. If you don't have the

Lawn Crack Profitability Calculator already, it is free, and you can get it on the resources page at LawnCrack.com. This tool will make it very easy to see how small changes in your business' numbers will affect your bottom line. Most small businesses fail because they fail to understand the basic financials of their business and industry as a whole. What is the cost per man hour to provide each offered service? How long does each service take to complete? What is your capacity per day? Per week? Per Year? How long is the working season in your area? And finally, you must know what your target profit is. Knowing these five things can help you determine exactly how profitable your business will be and get you a realistic overview of how much work, time, and money will be needed to accomplish this. This can change over time as you hire more skilled employees and can purchase more efficient professional equipment, so you need to reassess this from time to time.

Here is what I mean:

Let's keep it simple. Let's start with only offering a lawn mowing service and you, the owner, as the only employee. We will use $50 as the average mow price. And yes, $50 is going to be a very realistic number for your average mow price. I know pricing varies in different parts of the country, but in my area, this is very realistic. In the Midwest, where I operate my business, we average around 30 cuts per year on a typical property. If we use the $50 per cut price, times the 30 cuts per year, we will get $1500. That means for every $50 mowing account you pick up, you can expect to earn $1500 per year from that account. In other words, a $50 mowing account has a gross yearly value of $1500 to your company. I hope you are getting excited! These numbers add up quick!

Now we have the value of an average mow customer per year. Next, we need to know how many lawns you can cut per week. You will be able to cut many more lawns with a 60" zero turn as compared to a 21" push mower. This is why you will need to upgrade your equipment to professional grade equipment as quickly as possible. I will give you two scenarios right now for you to consider. I will reference back to these scenarios a couple times throughout the book.

Scenario 1 – You have a 21" push mower. You can cut five lawns a day, five days a week, and you cut these 25 lawns 30 times in a season.

25 lawns per week at $50 each is $1,250 per week. $1,250 per week times 30 weeks = $37,500. In my area, the season is roughly nine months long, so your gross income in this scenario is $37,500, and you still have three months per year to generate more earnings in some other way. If for some reason, you are satisfied with this amount of money and three months off per year, I would advise you to do business as a sole proprietor and not carry insurance. You are already making more money than most American's with this micro business. In reality, in this scenario, you own a job. A business must be able to operate without the owner's daily involvement to qualify as a business.

Scenario 2 – In scenario 2 we are going to use a 52" walk behind lawn mower on most lawns. You are going to want to keep your push mower to get in smaller gates though! You can cut 12 lawns a day, five days a week, and you cut these 60 lawns the same 30 times in a season. 60 lawns per week at $50 each is $3000 per week. $3000 per week times 30 weeks = $90,000. The season is still roughly nine months long, so your gross income in this scenario is $90,000, and you still have three months per year to generate more earnings some other way. The crazy part is, the time it takes you to cut 12 lawns with a 52" is going to be about the same as cutting five lawns with a 21" push mower. Call me crazy, but I would do whatever it takes to get a larger mower and open the door to this type of productivity, which translates to more dollars in my bank account. You still own a job, but now you are bringing in some pretty good money and hopefully see the potential to add crews and expand your income potential.

In scenario 2 you will have more costs, but you will still net more money at the end of the year. Did you know you can get a loan for a commercial mower with no money down? If not, it is true and at the time I wrote this, almost every lawn mower manufacturer is offering 0% interest for 48 months. A $6,000 walk behind is going to cost you $125 per month. You can cut $125 worth of grass every day before 10:00 AM if you want to. I had to put how cheap the equipment is in perspective here. Now that you have a larger mower, you will probably need a trailer too, although you could just use ramps to get the walk behind in and out of the bed of your truck. It would be wise to bite the bullet and get insurance now. You never know what could happen while driving from stop to stop, or driving the larger mower on your customer's property. You are making $90k per year now, pay the $1k to $3k per year to ensure that if something terrible happens, you won't be paying for it out of pocket. That is the point of having insurance!

Before we get too far along, I want to clarify a couple of things. The first is gross income compared to net income. The way I remember this is gross is gross because it is what you would have received if you didn't have to pay taxes or spend money to earn the income, and it makes me feel sick in my stomach. On a paycheck, gross would be the amount before taxes are taken out and net would be the amount after taxes are taken out. In your business, gross is the amount of income your company takes in, and net is the amount that is left once all associated expenses have been paid.

I also wanted to touch on owning a business versus owning a job. You will more than likely start off in this industry owning a job. There is nothing wrong with this, even if it is the ultimate goal of your business. All this means is that you do everything in your business, or the majority of the critical tasks, and your business would cease to operate if you were not there completing the tasks yourself. You can have employees and still own a job. A business can function without the presence of the owner. Businesses have systems in place for the employees to follow to complete each aspect of the work. Minimal time is required from the owner to operate their business if they desire. If you can run your lawn care business based in Kentucky from your beach front condo in Florida, you own a business. If you can't take a 10-day vacation until your season is over, you own a job.

I would like to provide you with some motivation moving forward. Each of my 2-man crews mow $110k worth of grass per year. Before I decided to change my business model, I had three of these crews out every day, along with two landscape crews, and a spray truck. Now we are getting into some interesting numbers which will allow, you as the owner, to make a comfortable living. This is why I encourage you to think big! Why limit yourself to $37.5k per year with a push mower and you doing all the work yourself? It just doesn't make sense. Just because most of the people in the world are satisfied, or at least seem to be because they don't do anything else to generate more money and are happy with $30k per year, does not mean you should be too. Don't compare yourself to others. Most people will never reach their full potential. Set your goals high and make it happen. I am reading another Grant Cardone book as I am writing this titled, Be Obsessed or Be Average. Read that and tell me it doesn't get your blood pumping!

To make this book easier to follow and understand I will be using a simple model of a company that only offers a lawn mowing service. I will go into the different aspects to consider if your business offers other lawn and landscape services later in the book. My company has done them all. Whether you want to take the advice in this book or not will not affect my future success, but it could very well have a positive effect on yours. Like any other knowledge you accumulate, what you learn in this book will do absolutely nothing for you if you do not take action and implement it in your life and business. I know you can and will. Please always feel free to reach out to me if you ever get stuck.

Chapter 1 - Action Steps

1.– Set clear goals for your business. I recommend starting with your 5-year goal and work backward to get your 3-year goal, then 1-year goal, and then quarterly goals. See the references at the end of the book for tips on how to effectively set goals.

2.– Write down your business plan. Using the SBA.gov tool will make this much easier and less intimidating. If you don't have a plan, by default, you plan to fail

3.– Use our Profitability Calculator to play around with the numbers. You can gain great insight from doing this and set realistic expectations.

CHAPTER 2

Make your Business Official - Business Structure

Before we get into industry specific advice, we need to keep everything on the up and up. If you already have your business formed, bank accounts set up, all licenses filed, and insurance policies in place, you could potentially skip to the next chapter. I encourage you to review this section though as there is valuable information contained within. You will need to form a business entity. You may want to consult a local lawyer, but it is not necessary. Your choices are to operate as a sole proprietor, a general partnership, an LLC, or an S-Corp.

The simplest and least expensive way to start your business is by being a sole proprietor. Operating as a sole proprietor means that you are conducting business as yourself. You will file an assumed name for your business with your state. This will be your DBA, or doing business as, and is also referred to as a trade name or fictitious name. While this is a viable business entity, you need to be aware of some downfalls with this model.

The major downfall with conducting business as a sole proprietor is that you and the business are one. If someone sues your DBA, they are, in fact, suing you. This could put all of your personal belongings at risk if you were to lose in a law suit. I have never been sued in nine years of running my lawn care business, but America is a sue happy country, and a lot of people would rather sue for money than work for it. It is aggravating, but it is the way it is. If you choose to operate like this, you know the possible consequences. Knowing this information, I still do not think it is that bad of an idea to start as a sole proprietor if you are the only employee, do not have a trailer, and do not use commercial grade equipment. You can switch to an LLC at any time.

Another business entity you should not use is a general partnership. A general partnership has all of the same downfalls as a sole proprietor, but now you have the liability of your partner getting sued and taking your business down with him or her. Not only that, but I do not recommend forming a partnership, even if in the form of a multi-member LLC, if you do not fully understand the terms and conditions of your partnership agreement. You will want a lawyer to draw up, or at least review, your partnership agreement. I have heard far too many horror stories of one partner contributing far more than the other partner, but they both get compensated equally because of their partnership agreement. Getting out of a business partnership is similar to getting a divorce. It will be just as expensive, if not more, and will be equally mentally draining for all parties involved.

An LLC, or Limited Liability Company, is more than likely going to be the best fit for a new lawn care business. As the name implies, an LLC does offer some protection to the members or managers assuming everything is set up and documented properly. Negligence on the part of the LLC owner, while conducting business, can put your personal items at risk in a law suit. Also, signing documents in your personal name, instead of as a member of your LLC, can allow the corporate veil to be pierced. 'Piercing the veil' is when the court determines for a particular reason that the protection offered by the LLC will not be enforced, allowing the plaintiff to go after your personal belongings as well as the business' belongings in the law suit.

There will be more fees associated with maintaining your LLC as compared to a sole proprietorship, but if everything is done right, you will receive much better protection. Make sure you run a name availability check in your state to make sure the name you pick for your business is available and not taken by another existing business. If you do plan on becoming a large company operating in multiple states, you will want to make sure the name you want to use is not trademarked.

Once you get to a certain revenue level, you will probably want to consider an S-Corp as your business entity. You can elect to have your LLC treated as an S-Corp by having your Certified Public Accountant (CPA), file a form with the Internal Revenue Service (IRS). You will want to discuss this move with you CPA to determine if it is right for you. At a certain point, switching to an S-Corp will save you money on taxes. My business elected to be taxed as an S-Corp around the $300k in revenue mark to give you an idea.

If you grow to a large company doing millions and millions in revenue each year, then you can consider incorporating.

You will need an EIN, which is an Employer Identification Number, to set up an LLC. You can do this for free at www.IRS.gov. You will need to do this even if you are the only employee. You will use this number in place of your social security number. It is essentially the SSN of your business. This is good because it further separates you from your business entity.

Forming an LLC is completed at the state level. The state in which your business is located. You will need to check with the cities and counties you will be working in to get properly licensed to do business there. Each city and county require additional licensing. If you are performing work out of state, you need to get properly set up with that state, and the cities and counties there too.

If you are conducting business out of your house to start, you will need to apply for a home occupation license. In my experience, this is not difficult to do and permission is usually granted. Depending on your Home Owner's Association (HOA) or neighbors, it may turn into a big deal. I operated my business out of my house with no issues until I had employee cars lining the streets. The city contacted me, and I moved my business down the street to a warehouse in the commercial district. It wasn't that big of a deal, but the rent expense and other related costs of renting the space increased my overhead by $1,000 per month.

You will need to set up a business bank account. You need to keep your business' money and your personal money separate. If you are an LLC, you will need to bring a copy of your EIN and Articles of Organization to the bank to do so. Articles of Organization is the document from your state officially showing you have formed an LLC. It would be great to put some money in your account now if you have it and can afford to do so. You will want to get checks and a business credit card. I highly recommend managing your money and using a credit card to pay for every business purchase you can. I have taken vacations each of the past several years using only the points my business credit card generated to fund them. Many banks and credit cards are offering incentives for opening new accounts. Check the references for links. I just got $200 for opening a business checking account and $300 for getting my business credit card with Chase Bank. There are usually some requirements to meet to get the incentives, but they are often very easy to meet.

While at your bank, ask about their payment processing service. You will want to accept credit cards. I prefer my customers to pay by credit card instead of by check. This will open your services up to a much larger pool of customers, as many people prefer to pay by credit or debit card. People also spend 18% more on average when using a credit card. Paymentech is Chase Bank's credit card processor and who I use for all of my businesses. You do not have to use your bank's payment processor though. Independent payment processors may or may not offer you better terms. If you are not ready to spend the little bit of money to get this setup, no problem, you can do this at any point. Just realize you are limiting your potential customer base to people willing to pay cash, by check, or money order. In my opinion, it would be very unprofessional for a lawn care company to ask to be paid by PayPal, or Venmo, or something similar. You need to act like a business if you are going to be in business.

We are almost through the technical stuff. The last three items I want to address here are insurance, workers comp, and Department of Transportation (DOT) regulations.

Worker's comp, or worker's compensation, will be required if you have employees who are not a part owner of your company. My best advice on worker's compensation is to get the cheapest policy that meets your state's minimum requirements. If you get into commercial work, large companies may require your worker's comp plan to exceed the state minimum to meet their requirements. Keep that in mind when you bid and adjust your bid accordingly. I have used nationwide providers for this as they were able to offer me the lowest rates. Try The Hartford or AP Intego as I have used both and they were both good choices. When you are just getting started, you may be required to get workers comp through your state's in-house government program. This is something you will have to research.

Everybody loves insurance, right? Well, if you didn't like insurance before starting your business, you are really going to hate it now! Again, if you get into commercial work, you will need to make sure your insurance limits meet the potential client's requirements. Before you get to that point, I recommend simply getting some quotes and talking to the agents about deductible limits and other factors that can raise or lower your insurance cost significantly. You will want to get a general liability policy for your business and commercial auto policies on your vehicles. You may also want to insure your equipment. I do, it is worth it to me. You can also get an umbrella policy if you would like. An umbrella policy would kick in and cover any claims over the limits of your other policies. It is a safeguard against a worst-case scenario. I never felt the need to get an umbrella policy in my business. These are all things you need to hash out with your insurance agent. Talk to people you trust to get a referral to a reputable insurance company. If you do not have a good referral, you are going to want to screen several companies and compare prices to find the best fit for you. I use State Farm and pay more than I would from other insurance agencies, but I know the owner personally, and the customer service and attention to my account are priceless.

Finally, time to discuss the dreaded DOT. The DOT, or Department of Transportation, is the authority regulating commercial vehicles in the United States. If you are conducting business and your vehicles are over 10,001 pounds, that includes the combined weight of your truck and trailer, you will need to comply with DOT regulations. Also, if your trailer is a tandem axle, you are required to get USDOT numbers even if under 10,001 lbs. Your company is assigned one USDOT number that will identify all vehicles with that USDOT number as belonging to your business. No one is going to tell you to get a USDOT number. Well, I stand corrected, the police will pull you over and tell you when they catch you. They may go ahead and fine you in the process. You will find the link to the official DOT website in the resources.

All states do not participate in this, but you do need to determine if you state requires compliance or not. Maybe you are one of the lucky ones to whom this does not apply. Big warning here: there are several fraudulent DOT services online. I fell for one once and had to get my lawyer involved to get my money returned. Only use information from www.fmcsa.dot.gov. This is the official site.

The only good news about USDOT numbers is that they are free! But do not get too excited just yet. Complying with the DOT is going to be an expense every year you are in business. First, it is mandatory to have your 'free' USDOT numbers put on your truck, along with your company name and phone number, and a number to identify each truck in your fleet. You can do this by using vinyl graphics or magnets. Next, anyone who will be driving a DOT vehicle must get a medical card by completing a DOT physical. Then you have the requirements for equipment that must be in your truck. This includes a fire extinguisher that is mounted, just having one in the truck in not good enough. You will also need emergency triangles, a first aid kit, and an accident log. DOT vehicles must also be inspected each year. If your vehicle fails the inspection, you will need to have everything fixed before you can use your vehicle again. Lastly, you will need to complete a pre-trip inspection before the truck goes out every day and log this data in case they ever want to see it.

So, hopefully, you are not too overwhelmed at this point. The DOT advice above is for vehicle 10,001 lbs. to 16,000 lbs. If you have vehicles larger than this, you will need to have someone with a Commercial Driver's License (CDL) operate the truck, and the requirements get even more strict. I am not super familiar with 16,001 lbs. and over DOT requirements, but for example, I know they need a spare headlamp in the truck and flares along with all the requirements previously stated. If your vehicles fall into this category, you will need to research the additional requirements.

Noncompliance with the DOT can lead to substantial fines towards the driver, the company, or both. A major violation is using a cell phone while operating a DOT vehicle. If caught, the fines are upwards of $10,000. I make sure my employees fully understand this and you should too. They can fine the driver personally and the company for the same violation. I don't know too many start up lawn care companies that could survive a $10,000 fine.

That is a wrap for the behind the scenes business requirements. Please don't let all of this information overwhelm you. There are all kinds of information online on how to get everything done, and honestly, it could very well cost you less than $1,000 to get everything completed correctly. Obviously, I do not know everyone's personal situation who is reading this book, but I almost hope you think $1,000 is a lot of money right now. What you are about to learn is going to open you up to a whole new world, and your relationship with money is about to get a lot better. Now, let's get to the fun stuff!

Chapter 2 – Action Steps

1.– Choose a name for your business and form a business entity. An LLC is the most common. If you have not already chose your business name, read the beginning of chapter 3 for advice.

2.– Set your business up to legally do business in all of the localities that you will be performing work in. States, counties, and cities will have certain requirements. Start with the state, then the county, and city if needed.

3.– Open your business bank account and get a business credit card. It is also a great idea to set up your merchant services now too so you can accept credit card payments from your customers.

4.– Get the insurance required to operate your business. A commercial auto policy for all company vehicles and general liability are the two types you should certainly get. Talk with your insurance agent about equipment insurance, disability/ income replacement, and umbrella policies.

5.– Workers Comp is only required if you have employees that are not part owner of your company. Once you hire your first employee, it is mandatory. Not having it can lead to fines, and even possibly jail time.

6.– DOT requirements. Make sure you understand and comply with the rules and regulations of the DOT. Their fines can put you out of business very quickly.

CHAPTER 3

Getting Started

Okay. So, if you have not already decided on a name for your business, you need to do so. As I mentioned earlier, check with your state's Secretary of State to make sure your name is available and not already in use by another company. I love this part of starting a business. Use your imagination here, but also use common sense. Think about your logo, the colors you will use, and your website's address. You want a name that is clever, memorable, and easy to spell. Keeping the business name as short as possible is also usually a good idea. Since you are unknown, it would make sense for your name to reference what your business does. You don't have the same clout as Coke or Pepsi just yet! When deciding the name of your company also consider coming up with a slogan now too. A slogan is a short, memorable tag line for business. You can change your slogan at any time if you would like as your business grows.

It is time to get some business cards. Hand your cards out to anyone who is willing to take them. Keep them in your truck because as you work, people are going to stop you and ask for a quote. If you can't help them right away, give them a card, and they can call later. It would be best to get their information, so you can contact them, you will get more jobs being proactive instead of reactive. Designing a professional business card is a must. Your business card should include your company name, your name, business phone number, business email, and your website. You may also want to list your services on the back of the card, or even offer a coupon. If you can't do graphic design work, use a service like Fiverr.com or UpWork.com to have a freelancer design your card for as little as $5. Your business cards must look professional and be made of a quality material. Make sure you pay a little extra to have your design printed on a thicker stock paper.

If you do not already have a website, business phone number, or a business email, do not worry. You will need to be able to solve problems if you are going to be successful in this industry. These are very minor problems. The truth about websites is that they are cheap, and I mean super cheap. If you have basic computer skills and are willing to learn, you can build your website yourself. It seriously will cost under $70 per year to own your site. I recommend building a WordPress website and using Host Gator to host it. If WordPress is too complicated, try Wix, it is more user-friendly and minimal technical knowledge is required. You can certainly use your personal phone number as your business number. I did this for almost six years until I freaked out when a customer sent me a text at 10:30 PM on a Sunday night. The next day I had a new personal phone and phone number!

If you are using your personal phone, don't forget to set up a professional voicemail greeting. A business email is free if you have a website, use Zoho.com to get yours or sync your business email to your Gmail account through your website's cPanel. You can also just get a yourbusinessname@gmail.com email, or whatever email service provider you prefer. My company still uses an @live.com email because websites were not nearly as popular back then as they are now. I didn't even have a website for the first couple years I was in business. You should not do this in today's day and age! You can, but it will slow your growth down tremendously.

At this point, I would not worry about a uniform for yourself or your employees, if you even have any yet. Uniforms are something you should get once you have some money coming in. Until then, wear well-fitting clothes without any offensive or inappropriate words or logos on them. I appreciate the collared shirt and khaki look for yourself or crew leaders, and even team members, but I am also a realist. When I was working in the field on a hot day, I wore black basketball shorts with my company t-shirt. Along with not spending money on uniforms just yet, I would also hold off on spending any money on miscellaneous marketing materials. But, even before getting some customers, you need to make sure you have all the needed equipment to perform the work.

When starting your business, my advice is to start off offering a lawn mowing service only. It will be the easiest way to pick up customers and have a recurring revenue stream coming in. If you get a mulching service only customer, you may not be back to this property until next year. After you build up your clientele, depending on your skill set, you may want to offer other standard services such as fertilization and weed control, mulching, pruning, and leaf clean ups. But, and this is a big but, I will tell you one of the mistakes I made in my company was trying to offer too many services. If you start off by only providing a mowing service as I advise, you will only need a lawn mower, a weed eater, a blower, trimmer string, some basic tools, and a couple of gas cans to get started. Another obvious thing you are going to need is a truck, and I highly recommend always wearing ear and eye protection while working too. The best noise isolating headphones double as hearing protection and also allow you to listen to audio books, podcasts, or music while you work.

If you have a car now, sell it or trade it in, and get a cheap, dependable truck. I started out putting my push mower and other equipment in the back of my mom's SUV. And it wasn't really my push mower either! It was a very humble beginning! All of my equipment was my parent's residential grade equipment they used to mow their grass. I had to plug their Craftsman electric hand-held blower into an outlet and drag around the extension cord to blow off my first several customer's properties.

If you start out only offering a lawn mowing service, you may already have access to all the equipment you need. You may maintain your property or could use your parent's, or another friend or family member's lawn care equipment. You will not be using this residential grade equipment long. You will need to invest, yes, invest in professional grade equipment as soon as possible. This is how you will make money, by completing many jobs efficiently every day, and you simply cannot do so with a push mower. Remember the vast difference in revenue generated in the scenarios used in the introduction of this book. The same amount of time was involved in producing the income, but using the larger commercial mower allows you to be much more efficient and profitable. You need to be smart about spending money, but you will need to spend money to make money in this industry.

Chapter 3 – Action Steps

1.– Pick a website domain, your business phone number, and business email.

2.– Get professional business cards designed and printed.

3.– Make sure you set up a professional voicemail, especially if using your personal phone!

4.– What specific services will you offer? You do not have to be the one-stop shop. You will grow much faster and healthier by limiting the services you offer.

5.– What equipment do you have and what do you need? Start with what you have and re-invest your earnings to upgrade equipment as fast as you can.

CHAPTER 4

Get Some Clients

Now you know my thoughts on getting started. Keep it simple by limiting the amount of equipment you need by only offering one or two services. You will be asked by customers to mulch, prune, and this and that. You need to stay focused and stick with the services you are set up to provide. I messed this up terribly, and it cost me several years before I reached the take home income level I desired. It discretely negatively affected my profit margins and I did not even notice. Network with other companies in your area. Find another small business that is getting started, or has been in business for a couple of years, that only mulches and prunes, or only treats lawns. You can sub the work out or refer your clients directly to them, and vice versa. You don't want the customer calling around because the random company that comes and quotes the mulch job has the potential to take your mowing business as well. Write out an agreement to be signed by both parties that is legally binding with the companies you partner with so they cannot take your customer for the service you are already offering if you go this route. Another word of caution here is that referring a company can reflect poorly on your business if they are not reputable.

I am getting ahead of myself a little bit! It is tough to sequence this book as so many aspects overlap and could happen in a different order. Everything you need to know is in here, and you can always come back to certain sections to reference information when you get to various points in your business. Remember, the action steps from each chapter can be found at the end of the book or by going to lawncrack.com/book-resources along with links to any product or service mentioned in the book. Actually, completing the steps and the learning more about what I am talking about in this book would be a great first step to implementing this information in your business. Only having this knowledge in your head will have very little benefit to your life or business, if any at all.

My first handful of customers came to me by word of mouth from friends, family, and co-workers. First, tell everyone you know that you are in business. You cannot be shy about this. Why should you be? Tell your family, friends, co-workers, and blast social media with it. This may or may not result in a couple of customers, but it needs to be done. I got a couple of accounts from people my parents knew by doing this, but I got a lot more by going door to door. Remember, you are just getting started. You should be doing everything you can for as cheap as possible. You need money to reinvest back into your business. You should have business cards, as I mentioned earlier, but now you will also want flyers.

I printed my first set of flyers from my parent's computer. I did splurge on photo paper though to give them that thick stock feel and the glossy look. I know, I'm fancy! In my flyer, I introduced myself and let them know I would love to earn their business. You can take this bit of advice from me, and I know it is cheesy, but it worked. I used a catchy, funny phrase to get people's attention while reading my flyer. It said, "Your lawn looks like it needs a haircut." That's it. People ate it up and next thing I knew I was to that 25 yards per week point I used in scenario 1.

Another way I would suggest getting accounts is by contacting the established companies in your area. If you have money to purchase accounts, you could indeed offer to do so if they had any they wanted to sell. But, often established companies are looking to become more profitable and have accounts that used to fit into their business model but no longer do. You may be able to pick up these accounts for free just by asking. If this attempt yields no new clients for you right off the bat, do not get discouraged. These companies do not look at you as competition yet, you have a long way to go before getting to that point. Before you hang up the phone with them, give them your contact information so they can pass it along to anyone who calls in that they do not want to service for whatever reason. To make this much more effective, mail them a thank you letter with some of your business cards, so they don't forget about you. Even better than mailing them would be to stop by their location and do it in person.

As you get started, you will need to be humble. Regarding my personality, I feel like an extrovert trapped in an introvert's body, but I only come off as an introvert. I am not comfortable talking to people I don't know and would rather not do it. My business would never have developed and progressed if I didn't get over this fear at least a little bit. I am much better at speaking to people in a business setting, which has been helpful. I also have become much better at talking to people I don't know, both on camera, and in person, as I forced myself into these situations repeatedly. If you never feel uncomfortable with what you are doing running and growing your business, you are not setting big enough goals or pushing yourself hard enough. I am not saying you should be out of control, but you need to be pushing yourself forward into new situations as you strive for greater success. It is natural to be uncomfortable as you have never done these things before. Most people will stay in their comfort zone all of their lives, and this is why they will never reach their full potential. I would rather die than live an average person's life. Average is one of my least favorite words. How do you feel about the word average?

It is feasible to get 25 customers in 1 weeks' time by going door to door for a couple of hours each evening. I believe most people feel they are above this, but this is a quick, simple, inexpensive way to get started. It would be best to do this in the spring, but in my experience, we sign up new mowing customers all season long. So, humble yourself and go door to door. If the owners are home, introduce yourself and tell them you would love to handle their lawn mowing needs. If they sign up, great! If not, thank them for their time and hand them a card. Move on to the next one. If no one is home, leave one of your funny flyers behind!

Now you have 25 clients, and this number is going to climb soon. Why? Because, assuming you do a good job, the neighbors are going to be asking you to cut their lawn too. By the way, doing quality work every service is mandatory. After all, your name and reputation will be on the line with every job performed. People these days are busy and cutting the lawn is a hassle, at least it is with home owner grade equipment! I think using the commercial grade equipment is a blast. If for some reason you are not planning on offering a high-quality service, please do us all a favor and get out of our industry, and stop reading my book.

Your business is beginning to grow. It is time to hash out some more behind the scenes business responsibilities to make sure everything goes as planned. I will go much more in depth on other advertising methods later, but we need to figure out routing, scheduling, invoicing, maintenance, and some other things before we worry about getting more clients.

Chapter 4 – Action Steps

1.– Get flyers made to advertise your business.
2.– Go door to door with your business cards and flyers. Give the people you talk to a business card and leave a flyer on the door if no one is home.

CHAPTER 5

Business Operations – Scheduling

Business operations is where we separate the boys from the men and the girls from the women. In my opinion, this is another area where most lawn care companies fail. Why would you be getting into this business if you did not like and were not good at performing the actual work? You wouldn't, or you are crazy, or you have capital and are planning on hiring employees do the labor from day one. It is an entirely different skill set to be good at the office side of a lawn care business as compared to performing the work in the field. I am confident that most people start their lawn care business in the same way I did. That would be by working for another company and learning how to do everything in the field before starting, but I know that this is not always the case. I know plenty of people who started their business without a clue how to do any aspect of it. So, even if you did learn how to mow, trim, edge, and blow properly. And you also learned how to sharpen the blades, change oil, check and blow out air filters, fix a flat tire, and I can go on and on. I bet the owner didn't have you there while he was making the schedule or invoicing. Damn, I'm good!

Scheduling

Let's talk about scheduling. I can't stress enough that you should get a software program to do this. I know guys who have $100k to $200k annual revenue companies still using excel spread sheets to route and schedule. I don't understand. There are free programs available like Yardbook. I started with Gopher 2006 and it cost me $100. Now I use Service Autopilot and recommend you do the same. Yes, I pay Service Autopilot hundreds of dollars monthly to use their program, but it saves me thousands of dollars monthly in time and wages. If you are serious about growing your business, please take my advice and start using Service Autopilot from day one as your customer relationship manager (CRM), invoicing, and scheduling program. It will not cost you hundreds per month as you don't have multiple crews in the field. Each crew leader will need the Service Autopilot app on their phone, and each mobile user will add to your cost. Service Autopilot understands our industry and that money will be tight as you get started. Their pricing reflects this to make it affordable for everyone.

Starting with the basics that may, or may not be common sense. I would like to think it is, but then I see the other companies in my area, and I am like, "Ugghhh, maybe it's not!" You need to cut lawns that are located near each other on the same day. It would behoove you to become very familiar with the roads in your area to allow yourself to create the most efficient routes. Before we even get to tightening up your routes, and trust me on this, only offer lawn mowing once a week or once every two weeks. That is every 7 days or every 14 days. You will not be able to accommodate people who want their lawn mowed every 10 or 12 days at scale. When you have 300 properties you are cutting on a weekly basis it is not going to be possible to make tight, efficient routes working in 10 or 12-day lawns. A quick note about every week versus every other week lawns, make sure you charge every other week lawns more money! It is going to take you more time to cut them. I refuse to leave a lawn looking bad and you should too. Every other week lawns will need to be double cut, meaning cut twice on the same visit, or you will have to blow around the clippings and clumps to make it look good. The customer needs to pay you for this additional time. Don't ever feel bad about giving someone an honest price for the work they want to be performed.

I was terrible about this when I got started. I wanted to give everyone a deal. That is crazy, and a great way to not make money. Even when you are just getting started you need to establish a minimum charge. My minimum charge is $45 per mowing service. I do not care how small the stop is. Every service we perform needs to cover the labor and materials required to perform it, along with drive time to get to and from the last and next stop, and cover its fair share of your company's overhead expense. When you are getting started your overhead may be low, but you need to account for future costs from the beginning. This will allow you to accumulate the money needed to buy the equipment and vehicles you will need in the future to grow your business. Never feel bad or guilty about making money in your business!

This is my best advice on determining what day of the week to cut each route. If you have commercial clients, cut them early in the week. We cut our commercial accounts on Sunday because there are fewer cars in the parking lot. This cuts down on trimming time as many of the cars in the parking lot overhang the grass and need to be trimmed under if we mow them during the work week. My guys like making money and get paid by the job, not the hour, so they are happy to do this as they make the same amount of money for cutting these properties in a shorter amount of time. I'll expand on performance pay versus hourly pay when I get to the employee section of this book. Most commercial places would rather have their grass looking recently cut throughout the week, so this works out well.

On the other hand, most home owners want their grass cut on Thursday or Friday, so it looks good for the weekend when they typically have more time to enjoy their lawn. With that said, I put my 'nicer' residential properties on Thursday and Friday routes, and the not so nice homes on Monday through Wednesday with any remaining commercial accounts. Of course, unfortunately, we do have some nicer lawns on our Monday, Tuesday, or Wednesday routes, I refuse to drive back across town to mow one or two nice lawns. You need to keep this in mind if you want to make money. If the customer is not okay with this, then they are not the customer for you. If you make everyone happy, you are probably doing something wrong, and losing money! I don't know about you, but I started my business to make money. I also had a passion for making lawns and landscapes look their best, and still do today.

Once you figure out which CRM platform you will be using, fill out your client's profile and get them on the schedule. As I stated before, you want to mow the lawns near each other on the same day. You do not get paid to drive. In fact, you lose money each second your truck is on the road. So, when you are going door to door, start with the surrounding neighborhoods closest to your start and stop point each day. This will probably be your house as you get started. My company is located in Kentucky just across the Ohio River south of Cincinnati. We never offered services to Ohio residents and our businesses did just fine. We do all our work in three Kentucky counties, with 95% of that coming from two counties and we only service the bordering edge of the third county. Crossing the river would have opened a whole can of worms, such as interstate travel with a DOT vehicle, Ohio taxes at the state, city, and county level, and an Ohio worker's comp policy. It was not worth it to me as there is plenty of work in Northern Kentucky, not to mention the heavy traffic getting across the bridge!

I almost left this paragraph out, but thought about it and included it even though I did make a statement regarding this earlier. You must do quality work, every single job, every single time. To some, this is so obvious, but I can tell you that some people do not understand this. We have lost long time customers because of one insignificant mistake made by the new guy on our crew on a single service. Customers are funny, and they are all unique. You will need to learn how to communicate with each client individually. It comes down to this very simple mantra, "Do what you say you are going to do, when you say you are going to do it, at the price you said you would do it for." If you do nothing else but this, you will reach some level of success. Lack of pride in one's work is rampant in today's society. I do not understand this at all and have always strived to be the best at everything I do in life and business. From my many interactions with other business owners, I know this is a common trait for people like us. When you start hiring employees is when you will really need to monitor this.

I have several properties subbed out at this point in my business, and I can tell you I have had to cancel most of my subs because they simply don't show up to do the work. It is unbelievable. Subbing out work is when you sub-contract another company to perform some or all of the work for your client. The client still pays you, and you then compensate the other company. The way I look at it is like this, the customer agreed on a price for me to provide the service, so now it is my duty to make sure it gets done week in and week out. I have heard every excuse in the book from my subs, and from talking to other company owners, as to why they couldn't get the work done on schedule. I promise you that your business will fail if you don't keep your end of the deal. It doesn't matter if it rained a lot that week, or you had plans on Saturday, no one cares. The customer will drop you and call the next company in a heartbeat. I specifically remember coming back to my house on one Sunday afternoon to a houseful of people partying at my house. I had planned the party, but mother nature didn't let me get the work done Monday through Saturday, so I was out there on Sunday getting it done. If you are not willing to make sacrifices like this, you may want to think of another business to start or keep your day job.

We do work outside. We are at the mercy of mother nature. If you are in the industry long enough, you will eventually experience a week where it rains seemingly every day. In these cases, communicate to your customers that attempting to mow their lawn will do more damage than good until the ground has time to dry. Let them know you will be out next week and will get everything back under control and looking good. Some customers will appreciate a skipped week as it saves them a little money and other customers will want it mowed no matter what. Get to know your customers preference in these situations so if you can only fit in a limited number of lawns one week, you know which ones to prioritize. This is also applicable over the summer when the growth rate of the grass slows down. Ask the customer what their preference is in these situations. I have found the most typical response will be, use your judgment. I like it like that as we don't need to check with anyone, we can assess the lawn and make our own decision on the spot. I personally never liked mowing a lawn that didn't need to be cut anyway.

Once you have a large customer base, it will be important that your scheduling program makes it easy to adjust the schedule. Once again, Service Autopilot has this covered. There will be several weeks throughout the year where you get rained out a single day of the week. Be sure your company can still complete the workload for the week in these situations. If your employees can work on weekends, filling up the schedule Monday through Friday may be okay. If they cannot, you may want to leave a half day open during the week, so you can complete the workload even if something like rain or equipment failure sets you back.

Chapter 5 – Action Steps

1.– Get a CRM software you can grow with. This will keep track of all of your customer's information along with providing you a way to schedule, route, and invoice efficiently.

2.– Schedule your jobs by location. The tighter your routes, the more money you will make. Commercial places should be at the beginning of the week and your 'nicer' residential lawns should be towards the end of the week if at all possible.

CHAPTER 6

Business Operations – Invoicing

Alright, so we have some customers and we have them in our CRM which lets us know when they are due to be cut again. Now we need to get paid! When you are just getting started with a handful of accounts, I would suggest invoicing after each mow. You need your money fast to keep your small business running. If the work is complete, ask to get paid. This would be a daily invoice scenario. When I started out I was not hurting for money as I worked full time for the lawn and landscape company I mentioned earlier and I still lived with my parents. I wasn't flush with moncy by any means as I started with a push mower, a home-lite curved shaft weed eater, an electric blower, and still lived with my parents at 24 years old! To keep it simple, I invoiced at the end of the month. If you can swing monthly invoicing at the beginning, go for it. It will consume much less of your time invoicing monthly as opposed to daily, unless you get Service Autopilot or a similar program, then invoicing takes 30 seconds each time you do it. That is how Service Autopilot pays for itself among other time-saving features.

If your customer will allow you to invoice by email, do it! I have now started charging my clients for paper invoices. It is 2018, there is no reason anyone should not have an email. I do not care how old they are! This is the only planet we can live on, and there is no reason to waste the trees on lawn service invoices. I charge $2.50 per paper statement and do not feel bad about it at all. Here is why. First, the stamp costs 49 cents. I also had to buy paper, ink, and an envelope, not to mention the time it took me to print, stuff, stamp, and mail the damn thing. Invoicing by email is free, better for the environment, and takes a fraction of the time.

Have you ever noticed that almost every business you can think of makes it really easy for you to pay them? Well, guess what, you need to do this too! That is why I suggest getting set up to accept credit cards from the get go. People also spend more when using a credit card because they do not feel the same sense of loss as when they spend cash or a check. Either way, they see the money exit their bank account faster than if they had paid you with a credit card. I seriously prefer to get a credit card payment over a check. Going to my PO Box, getting the checks, opening them all, entering the check numbers and amounts into my CRM, stamping the back, adding them up, and taking them to the bank is much worse to me than paying a 2-3% credit card processing fee. Credit card payments deposit into my account the next business day, and I don't have to do a thing because it syncs with my CRM automatically.

While on this invoicing and payment topic, I want to make sure you understand a reality that has happened to everyone I know who owns a business. Some people are not going to pay you! I know! If you are a decent person, this just seems absurd. But it is going to happen if you allow your customers to pay you on their own accord after the work is complete. I have developed ways to limit this from happening though. I can't say I would exactly recommend implementing this policy as you start your business because it will deter some people from doing business with you. In my opinion, anyone who won't do business with you because of this, are the same ones who were not planning on paying anyway. I created a policy that made the customer choose between prepaying for services or letting us hold their credit card on file for us to run after each service is complete. They can either pre-pay or auto-pay. I offer small discounts to incentivize people to do this. And yes, I account for the discounts when I quote the jobs, so I don't lose any money doing this and the customer thinks they are getting a better deal.

If you allow customers to pay at the end of the month or count on them to send you a check after each service, you will need to stay on top of your AR. AR stands for accounts receivable. If someone goes into a department store and gets caught stealing $300.00 or more worth of merchandise, they get charged with a felony. If someone refuses to pay your $2,000 invoice for services they agreed to and you have already performed, the court system will not help recover your money and they will not face any criminal charges. I will be lobbying to change this in my later years, but as it stands now, it is the way it is. Even if you take them to small claims court and win, the court system will not force them to pay. You do have the option to go back to court and request the court garnish their wages, but this may or may not even be possible. Oh, by the way, these two court dates to get to this point will cost you somewhere in the neighborhood of $200, and that does not include lawyer fees!

This topic gets under my skin. I have written off over $30k of bad debt in the eight years of running my business. It still makes me a little sick to my stomach, but I am a big boy and don't let it affect me anymore. I did have some success with a collection agency I found down at the GIE Expo in Louisville. The GIE Expo is short for Green Industry & Equipment Expo. It is in Louisville, KY each October. I highly recommend you attend this event at least once. You will have a blast. Check it out at GIE-Expo.com. The company is APR, which stands for American Profit Recovery. They have collected 10's of thousands of dollars for me over the past couple years for a very reasonable fee. They have the power to ding the credit of the debtor if they do not pay and you have all the invoices to back up your claim. I would consider this or consider filing a lien on the property instead of small claims court to collect bad debt. These options are less expensive and are more effective. A final thing to consider is filing a 'theft of services' charge against them. I am not familiar with this, but recently found out it may be an option to consider. Dealing with these situations is no doubt one of the worst parts of running a service based business. You need to be running your business, not in and out of court, so do everything you can to limit these situations from every occurring in the first place.

Chapter 6 – Action Steps

1.– How will you invoice? Daily, weekly, monthly? By mail or email? This is something you want to have figured out before the time comes to do it!

CHAPTER 7

Business Operations – Bookkeeping

Bookkeeping is critical to running a successful business. You should have your separate business bank account(s) set up at this point. You cannot co-mingle your personal and business money. It will get you in trouble with the IRS, and that is the last thing you want. I believe you should consult an accountant even before you begin doing business. I will use accountant and CPA interchangeably throughout this section. CPA stands for Certified Public Accountant. Please heed my warning about CPA's! They are not all created equal, and some are even down right terrible at their job. Do not take picking out an accountant lightly. It took me 7.5 years in business before I found a high-quality accountant who was a good fit for my business. I cannot describe how liberating it was when this happened. A good accountant will keep you in the clear with the IRS, and they can seriously save you money. I encourage you to start looking at money in a new way. Every dollar you have can be spent on something that makes you more money, an asset, or it is spent on something else that never comes back to you at all, a liability. Obviously, you need to eat and a place to live, but outside the necessities when you are in business, you need to only spend money on things that will make you more money. Like a good CPA, like Service Autopilot, and like that 52" walk behind mower.

I don't think anyone would disagree that QuickBooks would be an excellent choice for your bookkeeping. There are other options though such as Xero or FreshBooks. I would use whatever your accountant suggests. Although you can invoice through QuickBooks, I would recommend doing this through your CRM. As you already know, I recommend Service Autopilot which conveniently syncs with QuickBooks.

When you are in business, you need to track every dollar that comes in and goes out of your business. And by every dollar, I literally mean every single dollar. That is why using these programs is so important. Although tracking every dollar seems like a daunting task, it is actually one of the simplest parts of running my business. I will tell you exactly why. Like I said earlier, my company pays for anything and everything we can with a credit card. All of my crew leaders and managers have their own company credit card. Just to be clear, I pay my credit card balance off every month. I never carry a balance and never will. Check out the INK Card from Chase. By the way, I love Chase bank if you need a bank. The stuff that we can't pay for with a credit card is set up for online bill pay through my bank or I will write a manual check to purchase it. These are the three ways my business spends money. They are all tracked to the dollar by my bank. My bank syncs with QuickBooks and bingo, every dollar we spend has been accounted for, and I didn't do a damn thing. If you are making purchasing with actual cash money, you will need to document this very well. Receipts for any and all purchases should be saved in a file, or better yet, scanned into a computer. The IRS can request to see actual receipts dating several years back in your business. If you cannot supply them, you will have no defense against their allegations and will be subject to paying whatever they determined your underpayment to be along with fines and interest.

Tracking every dollar that comes in is almost as easy. Credit card payments are automatically synced to the customer's account in my CRM and then synced to QuickBooks from there. All checks received are manually allocated to the proper account in my CRM and then also synced to QuickBooks. All cash goes right into my pocket, and I delete the invoice like the job never happened! Just kidding! I had to see if you were still paying attention. You could, in theory, do just that. I am not going to recommend or condone that behavior in this book though. I would rather pay a couple of extra dollars in taxes than risk an audit or worse, tax evasion. As much as I do not like paying taxes, I do like paved roads and other things that we take for granted in the United States. I swear there are pot holes in the Jamaican roads that will swallow your car if you are not paying attention!

A good accountant will legally reduce your taxes to the smallest amount possible. Another reason you need to consult an accountant is because of depreciation. Several items you will be using in your business will need to be written off over a period of years determined by their useful life. The IRS has a schedule to let everyone know how many years certain items should be depreciated. If section 179 of the IRS code is still an option going into the future, you can write off your entire purchase in the first year. You will need to discuss the pros and cons of this with your CPA. Items that need to be depreciated include mowers, vehicles, computers, and customer lists, among many others.

One last thing I wanted to include about accountants and preparing your taxes is that you are still ultimately responsible for the accuracy and timely delivery of your tax payments and paperwork. Yet another reason why it is so crucial to find a good one!

Chapter 7 - Action Steps

1.– Get with an accountant and pick an accounting software.

2.– Make a plan with your accountant on how to track all of the money coming in and going out of your business.

CHAPTER 8

Business Operations – Maintenance

Hopefully, you have a better understanding of how to properly and efficiently route, schedule, and invoice your jobs, along with the importance of tracking the money coming and going from your business. The last topic I want to discuss in this section is maintenance. I did not take this too seriously at the beginning of my business, and I paid the price. Please learn from my mistakes. It ended up costing me, or my company, over $22k to replace three engines in my trucks over the years. I realize I am using the words we, me, or I, and my or our business interchangeably. Here is the reason why, at the end of the day businesses are really people. There is not a single business in the world without a person behind it. Although I am the sole owner of my business I would not have a business without everyone else in my organization. That is why I use these terms interchangeably.

Develop a schedule for maintenance to make this easy. Anything with an engine, blades, or grease fittings needs to be on your maintenance schedule. Reference your user manuals for each piece of equipment and set the schedule for maintenance accordingly. The biggest thing to check is going to be oil. Checking oil is so quick and easy it would not be a bad idea to check it daily, but at a minimum, it needs to be checked weekly. I bet this would have saved me from having to replace 1 or 2 if not all 3 of the engines I had to replace. One of them had 197k miles on it so that one was probably toasted no matter how often I checked the oil. Other items to attend to on a regular basis are grease fittings and air filters. On a less frequent basis, hydro oil, belts, and fuel filters will need to be changed as well.

A huge deal when cutting grass professionally is sharping the blades on your mowers and scraping the decks regularly. How often you need to do this will depend on several factors which include how much use each mower gets, the type of grass you are cutting, and the height of the grass you are cutting. We sharpen our blades every other day most of the year. Over the summer, sometimes we can go every three days, and in the spring, we may need to do this daily. If you are paying attention to your cut quality, you will notice a significant decline in quality when your blades begin to dull. Check out our tutorial on how to do this properly and in as little time as possible on our LawnCrack YouTube Channel. Dull blades will tear the grass blades instead of cutting them. This will damage the turf and can even leave a white tint to the lawn as the torn grass blade tips die off over a period of days after you cut the lawn. Every time you sharpen the blades you need to scrape the buildup of clippings from underneath your mower deck. You have probably noticed the fins on your lawn mower blades. These fins create lift, much like an airplane wing, which draws the grass up as the mower runs over it. This is what gets you a nice flush cut. If you have you deck caked with debris, this lift is not created, and you end up with an uneven and very unprofessional cut.

Although keeping your equipment in as good of condition as possible is not necessarily maintenance, it will certainly lower your maintenance costs. I have never understood the guys that leave their equipment outside to bear the elements while it is not in use. The useful life of the equipment will be dramatically reduced, and you will begin having issues with it way before you ever should. If you don't have a shelter of some sort, at the very least bungee a tarp down over your equipment to keep rain, snow, and sunlight from degrading it prematurely. In my area, leaving your equipment out is also a good way to get your stuff stolen.

I rarely see owners damaging their equipment, but I have worked with and employed people who felt it was okay to throw a trimmer if a rock happened to smack them in the face. Or instead of gently lowering a blower down out of the flat bed, they drop it and crack the housing. Or the classic, let's throw rocks in this plastic wheel barrow and see what happens! I will cover the importance of an employee handbook when I get to employee section later in the book, but mine clearly states if they are negligent with the operations of the equipment resulting in it needing to be repaired or replaced, that expense will be their responsibility. This is not to get misconstrued with Johnny was using the 7-year-old trimmer when it finally crapped out, so he owes me a new one.

Chapter 8 – Action Steps

1.– Set a schedule of when maintenance items will be performed, along with a schedule to check fluid levels, etc. on a regular basis.

CHAPTER 9

Business Operations - Position Yourself for Growth

We have covered getting your business set up properly, how to get your first customers, how to schedule, how to invoice, what you need, the importance to upgrade your equipment as fast as possible, and maintaining your equipment. The very best way to learn anything is by doing it. Once you are comfortable with how to do all of the aspects of your business, it is time to grow. It is essential to get these basics down before even thinking about growth. If you grow too quickly, I can almost assure you that you will fail. Failure is something you will encounter regularly when growing your business. This is not to be feared. Each failure provides an excellent opportunity to learn what does not work and how you could improve on it in the future. One thing is for sure though, if you fail to plan, you plan to fail.

I want to discuss how to systematize your business. I don't think everyone has grasped the importance of systems in their business. Systems will be the life blood of your business and could very well be the one factor determining just how successful you will be in business. I read The E-Myth Revisited by Michael E. Gerber twice before starting my business, and it would be ignorant for you not to do the same. I know my word choice is a little harsh here, but I wanted to make sure you didn't just skip pass that recommendation. Get Audible and listen to the book while you work. Honestly, The E-Myth Revisited is the only book I have ever read in my life, but I have listened to over 100 books while working in my lawn care business using Audible. You can get your first 2 audio books for free by using the link in the resources section or on LawnCrack.com.

I am happy to say that I am now reading Think and Grow Rich at the time of writing this book. I had listened to it twice previously, but it was brought to my attention that this is a book that is best read. That turned out to be sound advice. You should highlight words and phrases in the book that sound out to you and reference them often. Think and Grow Rich by Napoleon Hill contains the secret of how to obtain whatever it is you desire in life. If that is not a good enough reason to read the book, I don't know what is. Napoleon dedicated 25 years of his life to studying the 500 wealthiest people in American at the time which the early 1900's. The principles of success he documented in the book are truly priceless and timeless. I think it is an absolute shame that book is not taught in our school systems.

So, what the hell do I even mean by systematize your business? In its essence, systematizing your business is the process of documenting how each individual aspect of your business is to be performed. Every successful business in the world does this without exception. Mr. Gerber references McDonald's in The E-Myth Revisited, and he could not have picked a better example. No matter where you go in the country, or even the world, if you go into a McDonald's and order a Big Mac, you are going to get the exact same sandwich. The meat patty will be the same weight, and the exact number of toppings will be uniform with any other Big Mac. So how does this relate to your lawn care business?

This is how. No matter what crew goes and cuts a lawn on your route. The finished product should be the same, which is a perfectly mowed lawn. I can't go into detail on exact steps for every system in this book, but I will offer several examples of things you need to systemize. I will use mowing a lawn as an example to show you what I mean.

Using the lawn mowing service example, the following is a great system. I will use a 2-man crew for this example as I feel that is the most efficient and safe number of people to have on a crew. I do believe a 1-man crew can produce more profit than any other, but I do not like having employees out in the field running mowers by themselves. Some things are in fact more important than making money, but not many! Safety is one of them. Anyone driving a commercial vehicle needs to have a heightened sense of awareness and responsibility to keep everyone else on the road safe. Often our vehicles are big and heavy and can cause a lot of damage very quickly if operated carelessly. Operating the lawn mowers, especially zero turn mowers on hills, chain saws, hedge trimmers, and even string trimmers can cause serious injury or death too to the operator or people nearby. Never get to comfortable using the equipment and reiterate this to your employees on a regular basis.

Here we go with the 2-man mow system example. The truck pulls up and parks in a safe location, not blocking any driveways or fire hydrants, or anything like that. The crew leader logs the start time of the job, and the crew gets out of the truck immediately. Depending on the size of the property, both crew members will begin mowing, or one will begin mowing while the other starts to trim and edge. The person mowing should outline the property blowing all of the grass away from obstacles. Once the property is outlined, the mower should then section off the lawn and stripe it up. The trimmer should start at the front right of the property by the street. He should trim and edge his way along the sidewalk, up the drive way, around the house, and then finish as he started on the left side of the property by the street. Everything should be trimmed and edged in one efficient path around the property. Whoever gets done first grabs the blower and begins blowing the property off starting at the street and working their way to the back of the property. Both team members quickly double check to ensure everything has been completed, quality standards were met, no tools are left behind, and everything is securely back on your truck or trailer. They then immediately get back in the truck, clock out of that job, and drive to the next stop.

No matter who is on the crew, they should know this is how to mow a lawn correctly. If a customer is watching different crews mow their lawn each week, they should not be able to tell that anything is different. The process to complete the job was done the same exact way, and the result is a professionally mowed lawn every time. I highly recommend having the same crew mow the same properties each week if possible though. The employees seem to like a routine better than random lawns to cut each week and the customers definitely appreciate seeing the same faces on their property each week. This also makes it easier for the crew leader to determine faster routes to take from stop to stop over time if he is constantly running the same route.

A good thought to instill in your employee's mind is to conduct themselves like the customer is watching them at all times. Items they should be paying attention to include behaviors such as loitering, smoking on the customer's property, language choice, their tone of voice, body language, sneaking off to use the restroom, and use of their phone while working.

Anything and everything should have a system in your business. When a customer calls your business phone, whoever answers the phone should say the same exact thing. You should not have one person answer by saying, "Hello," and another person by saying, "Hi. Thanks for calling Your Company. My name is John. How can I help you today?" Side note about your phone, as I said earlier, make sure you have a professional voicemail message in case you cannot answer the phone. And a couple more side notes about the phone calls, voicemails, and even emails. Have someone pick up the phone if at all possible. This alone will make your company look better than at least half of your competition. The next best thing is calling or emailing people back promptly. Form the habit of calling or emailing people back at lunch, in the evening, or first thing in the morning if you are still out in the field. If you leave people hanging, they will find someone else to get their job done.

Back to systems. We already went over maintenance, but all aspects of your maintenance schedule should be systematized. From when each task is performed, to how you perform each task. You accounts receivable system should be a priority if you are allowing people to pay on their own accord after you provide a service. You need to decide when you will cut off service if payment is not received. Think about it. If you invoice at the end of the month on a weekly cut lawn, you have 4 or 5 cuts completed before you even send them an invoice. If you give them 2 weeks to pay, which is plenty of time, you will be 6 or 7 cuts in before they are even considered late with their payment. At $50 per cut, that is $300 or $350 you could be out if they don't pay you and this is just one account. Commercial accounts may even have net 30, net 60, net 90, or even longer terms. This means per the contract you have with them, they have 'X' number of days before payment is due. Be very careful of this. Cash flow is king and can crush a small business if not managed carefully.

Another system you should have in place is how you will react to slow pay or no pay accounts. Sometimes people may have honestly missed your email with the invoice attached, or maybe they did send in their payment, but it was lost in the mail. I have had several checks never make it to my PO Box. My point here is to start off assuming the best, that it was an honest mistake. Maybe start off with a friendly email reminder. If they don't respond within a day or two, give them a call. If they don't answer, leave a message. If these two attempts are ignored, consider mailing them an invoice and send another email with a more serious tone, but keep it professional. If none of these attempts get a response, it would be time to start whatever collection method you feel is best for this account.

Possibly one of the most important systems in your business will be your note taking system. If you are answering the phone as you are completing jobs, this is even more critical. How are you going to remember everything you need to do? What if you are on a large property and it would take several minutes to get back to your truck to write down the customer's information? It is a tough spot to be in. My way of handling this may not be the best and is certainly not the most technology advanced method out there, but it does work very well for me. I have all of my daily tasks wrote on a black piece of paper I keep on a clipboard. I make a new piece of paper for each day of the week and do my best to complete each task on the day it should be complete to avoid having to re-write it on the next day's sheet. If I am not near my clipboard when a thought pops in my head or I just spoke with someone on the phone, I email myself from my phone so as soon as I get back to my computer, I can complete the task or put it on my task sheet. If I need to take notes while still on the phone, I put it on speaker mode, and type out that email to myself while still on the phone with all the pertinent details. Evernote would be worth considering to help you keep up with your to-dos. I have heard a lot of great things about it, but have not started using it myself just yet.

A calendar of some sort is also going to be a major system you will need to implement as well. Any of your recurring tasks should be on your calendar. Although I really am a techy guy, once again I use a paper calendar on my desk to map out my upcoming events, responsibilities, and tasks. Every day I reference my calendar before I head out, any tasks due on that day make their way onto my task sheet that morning. Some examples of items you will find on my calendar include a payroll reminder each Monday, a note to run all credit cards we keep on file on Tuesdays, when quarterly tax payments are due, and any meetings I have set, among other items.

I think you get the idea on systems. I hope you see the importance if you are planning on growing your company. If your goal is to employ yourself, you can very possibly get by without them. I just want to let you know you are leaving a lot of money on the table in doing so, and you will be physically out in the field all season doing the work to come back to the office to do the office work each evening or every morning, or possibly both. Once again, this is owning a job, not a business. Not that this is the worst thing in the world or that anything is wrong with it. I think it is 10 times better than working for someone else. You are either creating your own dream life, or you are creating someone else's. Ponder that for a minute or two.

Chapter 9 – Action Steps

1.– Start documenting your business' systems. I know this may not seem important just yet, but doing this will set you up for success when you are ready to hire employees. Do a system or two a week and before you know it you will have a book of systems to show new hires so they can reference it instead of asking you as they begin to take over the responsibility of handling these tasks.

2.– Get a calendar system in place so you always know your upcoming responsibilities.

3.– Make a daily task sheet so you do not forget to complete any important tasks. Add to your task sheet throughout each day as new items present themselves that need to be attended to.

CHAPTER 10

Time to Grow – Marketing

This is an exciting time in your business. You are up and running. You are getting very comfortable with all the tasks involved in running your business and have begun to document your business systems for when you are ready to hire employees. By document, I mean write them down. Before you hire your first employee, you should have so much work that you cannot complete it by yourself anymore. The truth is you will need to do this to be able to afford an employee. No one said this was going to be easy. But if done right, it can be a lot of fun and make you a lot of money.

Marketing is hands down one of my favorite parts of any business. Marketing, advertising, and branding are fascinating to me, and I have spent a lot of time and money determining the best ways to do each. Without question, no doubt about it, my website has gotten me more customers than anything else. I have received small individual residential customers to large accounts such as FedEx from them simply visiting my website. I do know some old school guys in the industry with large successful companies that do not have a website. These guys have been in business since the 80's and are grandfathered in if you will.

Once you have been doing business in the same area for almost 40 years, a website may not be necessary for you, but until then, it is going to be one of your most valuable assets if done correctly.

I don't know how techy you are, but there are two crucial factors regarding your website. The first is that people can find your site by searching for it on the internet. This is referred to as SEO or search engine optimization. SEO is the art and science of providing the search engines with the information they need to know to know when it is appropriate to show your website in the search results determined by what the person types into the search bar. Typically, people will search for whatever service they are looking for in their city, not your company name. You want to make sure your site comes up when people are searching for what your company does, and they are in your service area. It is important to remember that the content on your site also needs to be appealing to humans who are viewing your site, not just the search engine algorithms. It is very important to remember to verify your website with Google and Bing, and Facebook requires this as well. If you do not get verified, they will not display your site or page in the search results nearly as often as they would if you had. If you need help with building your website or optimizing it for the search engines, contact Lawn Crack and we will get you a fair quote at LawnCrack.com. We special is building websites and general online presence for lawn care and landscaping companies.

The second vitally important characteristic of your site is UX or user experience. You need to make it super easy for anyone who lands on your site to know what you do and how to contact you. Put a contact form right on your home page for people to quickly and easily fill out in one minute or less to give you their information so you can provide them a quote. Also, have your phone number and email visible and easy to find in case they would prefer to contact you that way. Have your social media accounts linked here too. Everyone is different and offering more ways for people to contact will only benefit you. The last thing that relates to UX is making sure that your site renders correctly on a mobile device. It is imperative that your website also looks good and is fully functional on a mobile device as well as a computer, laptop, or tablet.

Take advantage of all of the free social networks we have these days. Obviously, the biggest one is going to be Facebook. Not only is this a free and easy way to keep your company in front of potential new clients and communicate with existing customers, but it also will help your website rank better in the search results. Even if you do not use the social platforms, creating and completing your profile will help you rank better. Another place you want to have all of your company information is on citation sites. These are sites such as yp.com, yelp.com, superpages.com, and many, many others. I suggest doing these yourself overtime, but there are services out there that can complete this for you. It is critical that your information on these citation and social sites is consistent. Mainly this refers to your business name, address, and phone number often referred to as your business' NAP. Inconsistent information across the web lowers your credibility in the search engines eyes, and they are less likely to rank your page.

Never forget your website will get more business for you than anything else ever possibly could. This is so true because all other methods of advertising you will use are going to direct people to your website! You can direct them to your Facebook business page or direct them to call, but if your site is designed properly, it will be a selling machine. Also, no one needs to be available to answer when someone visits your website. You will learn the more you can automate your business the happier you will be along with increasing your ability to profit. There is no point in accumulating money if you never have the time to enjoy it. Simplify and automate everything in your business that you possibly can.

Once you start developing relationships with some of your clients, ask them for a review. The best three places to request them to leave a review are on Google, Facebook, and Yelp. Bing uses the local business information from Yelp to populate their search results, and Yahoo is powered by Bing, so you get two for one in that deal. Reviews left on these three sites will yield you the greatest return. No matter where someone leaves you a review, even if just in an email, copy and paste that review to a page on your website dedicated to your reviews and testimonials. It would also be beneficial to sprinkle reviews across the other web pages on your site. My favorite place to put them is right above my quote request form, so they inevitably see them right before they request our services. It gets us started off on the right foot from the get go.

Your guarantee is something else that should be included in at least some of your marketing campaigns. In my experience, hardly anyone will ever take you up on your guarantee. So why not have one? It is another credibility builder, just like your reviews. My company's guarantee is, 'We are confident you will be blown away with our services. If for any reason you are not, please let us know and we will make it right. Or refund your money for the last service.' If you cannot confidently make that statement about your business, maybe you are in the wrong business!

If you have any association with or are certified by an authoritative entity, that would be another great credibility builder to insert here and there as you can too. The NALP is a great example. NALP stands for National Association of Landscape Professionals, which was formerly PLANET. I can't say you should join the NALP, as I did not get anything out of my membership when it used to be PLANET, but maybe I just didn't utilize my membership to its fullest potential. Your BBB, or Better Business Bureau rating, is another great one to include. If you are a Super Service awards winner from Angie's List, that would be worth displaying as well. There are several others that I do not include here.

Advertising is any method you use to market your business, such as your website, business cards, flyers, etc. Marketing is the actions you take to make people aware of your services. It is how you get their attention. Branding is making your company name and logo recognizable to your target market over time. Branding creates loyal customers, as well as loyal employees. Your brand is something to believe in and stand behind. It is how your business is perceived. You have branded your business when someone just catches a glimpse of your logo, and they automatically know that it is your business and what you do. That is where you want to get.

We haven't covered this yet, uniforms and graphics on your truck. In my opinion, as soon as you can afford either of these two things, you must get them. You want your customers to see one of your employees on their lawn or your truck in front of their house and know it is you. I would not expect to get much business from your uniforms, but this is part of being a professional. For the guys in the field, this could be as simple as a t-shirt, but I recommend getting them a hat and hoody too. As soon as you can, get yourself, the owner, and your managers and crew leaders, polo shirts and more formal jackets. Your truck logos, on the other hand, will, over time, start to generate you some new business. You can go crazy with a full wrap or as simple as a door magnet. It is up to you, your budget, and how you want to present your company to the world.

As your business grows, you need to continue to increase your advertising budget. We have talked about business cards, websites, and flyers earlier. The very next advertisement I would urge you to consider is yard signs. They are sometimes referred to as bandit signs and look like the political signs we all know and love each time election time rolls around. I like these so much because you can target customers by location very accurately. Place the signs at the entrances and exits of neighborhoods where you want more customers or at the end of an interstate off ramp where you want more customers. Remember, the closer your customers are to each other the better! You may want to check with city ordinances about the legality of placing these signs along road ways. I have never heard of anyone getting fined in my area, but I have seen city trucks removing signs before. If you leave them out long enough, someone is going to eventually throw them away. If you want to get the most out of your signs, simply swing by back the locations you placed the signs and pick them up a couple days later. That way you can reuse them. If you do want to collect the signs, make sure the grass is freshly cut where you place the signs because the mow crew responsible for that turf will more than likely pick it up as they mow.

You can certainly consider Google AdWords, Bing Ads, and Facebook ads. All of these platforms offer location targeting, and Facebook lets you get extra picky about who will see your ad. That is why advertising on these platforms is so popular and a multi-billion-dollar industry. They work. I highly recommend consulting an expert to set up these ads for you. We have tutorial videos on LawnCrack.com and the LawnCrack YouTube channel if you insist on doing this yourself. You honestly can waste a lot of money if your ad copy is not good, your pictures or videos suck, and you don't structure the ads properly with regards to targeting and keywords, etc. Copy simply means the word choice you use in your ads. Even if you want to do this inhouse, I would strongly suggest paying a professional to set up your first couple ads so you could then duplicate what they did in your future ads.

One of the biggest successes my company had with an advertising campaign was with an EDDM campaign we ran just before spring came one season. EDDM stands for Every Door Direct Mail and is a service offered by the US Postal Service. At the time of writing this book they will deliver each piece of mail for $0.177, so under 18 cents apiece. You can't even mail a post card for that! You need to have your mail pieces formatted correctly and abide by the handful of rules they have for this platform. But it is easy to navigate and get this done.

Here is my advice on doing a mail campaign of any kind. Make sure you send at least send one follow up piece to every address you target within 7-10 days of mailing the first piece. I would recommend sending three pieces to each house within a 3 or 4-week time frame, preferably in the spring right before everything starts growing and lawn care is on the top of everyone's mind. If you choose not to take my advice and send only one mail piece to each address, do not expect to pick up many customers. It may be a complete waste of time and money. We got very few calls from our first mail piece when we did this, but the second mailing brought in hundreds of calls and quote requests. If I were to do it again, I would send a 3rd piece to the same houses again. My campaign consisted of 20,000 pieces that I sent to the same houses twice. I did create 2 different mail pieces, but you could send the same one if needed. The only warning I have about doing this is to make sure the mail routes you choose do not have apartment or condo associations on them. This would waste a lot of money very quickly as these people do not handle their mowing needs, the association does.

Another option for targeting customers by mail is Radius Bomb. This is new and at the time of writing was not available in all locations. Radius Bomb allows you to very quickly and easily mail to certain houses by highlighting them on a map or by entering one of your customer's address and then selecting to have a mail piece sent to the surrounding homes. This is very exciting and just another reason why we encourage you to subscribe to our podcast and YouTube channel so you can be informed of these new tools as they become available. The world is changing at a rapid pace and it will be imperative for you to keep up if you want to succeed moving into the future.

If you get big, then you can consider running a radio or TV ad. Just keep in mind a lot of the people who hear or see these ads may not even be in your service area. Another thing to consider is the cost of broadcast ads. They will be the most expensive type of advertising you can do with little that can be done to track ROI, which is return on investment.

Tracking your ROI should be part of your marketing plan. If you are going to be spending money on obtaining clients, you should really find out what is working and what is not. That way you can stop using the low return advertising methods and concentrate your marketing dollars on the campaigns that are delivering the greatest return. The best way to do this is by asking each lead that contacts you how they heard about your company. My company integrated that question into our quote request form. If the lead calls in, we ask them during that initial conversation. Through trial and error, you can determine what works best for your company. Another way you could track this is by having people use a coupon code to let you know which advertisement they saw. With internet ads you have the option to split test, or A/B test, different ads. The platform you are using will alternate different ads you created and the analytics will let you know which one is performing better. Never forget the method of marketing you are using may be correct, although the pictures and copy of your ad may not.

Some other things to consider are getting novelty items with your company branding on them. This could be anything from magnets to pens, to frisbees, and the list goes on and on. I would be wrong not to include word of mouth here too. Word of mouth is when advocates of your business talk about your business to their friends, family, neighbors, and co-workers and you end up getting a new client from their conversation. Just remember word of mouth works 10 times better in reserve, meaning if you do poor quality work, word of mouth is not going to help you, but hurt you 10 times as bad.

You also have the option of using lead generation services. I recommend you proceed with caution here! Angie's List is probably the biggest one out right now. I advertised with Angie's List for two full years and will never do it again. The first year was actually okay, but Angie's List made a lot of changes and the quality of their leads has gone way down in my opinion. Also, it seemed every person that contacted us from Angie's List was extremely picky and a lot of them were down right unreasonable. There are several others such as Thumbtack, Nextdoor, and HomeAdvisor. I have heard of some people having success with these, but I feel there are much better, cheaper ways of gaining new clients than going any of these routes.

Lastly, in the marketing section, I want to touch on networking. This honestly gave my small business a big boost when I was just getting started. I did the unthinkable and joined a BNI group. BNI is Business Networking International. I am not a huge fan of BNI and certainly did not ever drink their Kool-Aid as everyone always says. I still don't even know what that means! But I connected with a realtor, a mortgage broker, an insurance agent, a roofing company's sales manager, and a lawyer very quickly in my BNI group. Those five guys didn't sell hamburgers, sorry, I couldn't help myself, but they did send me a ton of new business! As you may have been able to tell by now, I am not your average lawn care business owner. I am an entrepreneur, and my lawn care business was my first legitimate business. I tend to form relationships with people doing something with their lives, and it makes me get better at life and business whether I am conscious of it or not. Take a second and consider the five people whom which you spend the majority of your time. Inevitably you will slide up or down the success ladder depending on whether these people are doing better or doing worse than you in life and their overall mindset. BNI has a rigid structure making it very time intensive and does come with a monetary cost too. In my area, many business professionals have gotten fed up with BNI's rigid structure and started their own networking meetings.

If you ask around, I am sure you will find a free business networking meeting that will also not kick you to the curb for missing a meeting. I have found business coaches often organize quality networking meetings and are able to get a lot of people to them. Don't forget about networking with other lawn care and landscaping companies in your area, or even just outside of your service area. You can refer customers back and forth depending on which company could serve the client best. It turns out to be a win-win for everyone involved when done right. Please consider the fact that your reputation can be damaged by referring an incompetent company. I have stopped referring customers to other businesses for this reason. A lot of people running lawn care companies do not have a clue how to run a business. I don't think they are bad people or are doing it on purpose, I honestly believe they just don't know any better.

Jim Rohn said, "People would do better if they knew better." It is a sad truth that most people are too lazy to educate themselves these days. My self-education has brought more success, money, and free time into my life that I could have ever imagined. It is mind boggling to me that most people live pay check to pay check when only a small amount of specialized knowledge learned and applied could set them free. I can't stress enough how much I encourage you to listen to audio books instead of music while out in the field working. Please do yourself a huge favor and at very least get your 2 free audio books from Audible.

Concluding the marketing section, here is some solid advice on how to convert as many clients as possible. In all of your advertising messages be sure to make it clear that your service will solve a problem the potential client has or will fulfill a desire theirs. The images and words you use should help the person viewing your ad envision themselves using your service and how it will improve their life in some way. Make ads specifically targeted at families with small children and different ads for the folks getting older that can no longer maintain their lawns themselves. Doing this will increase your conversions greatly as opposed to throwing out a one size fits all advertising piece.

That last thing is your ability to quote these new requests fast. The longer it takes you to provide your quote, the less of a chance you have of signing that customer up. For any job that you can quote based off square footage such as mowing, lawn treatments, and aerating and overseeding, make a pricing guide that correlates to the square footage of their lawn. You can then use Google Maps and DaftLogic.com to quote these jobs from your computer. We often quote these services before hanging up the phone with the client. They are equally part impressed and part freaked out at the same time! It often leads to a new client on the spot. For mulch jobs, pruning, snow removal, and other services that you really need to see in person, let them know how long it will take you to get your quote together and then supply your quote in the time frame you specified.

Chapter 10 – Action Steps

1.– Get a professional website built that can be found by the search engines and that is very user friendly. This will be how you get the majority of your customers! Do not skimp out on this. Contact us if you need help with this.

2.– Make your social profiles for your business. Facebook is the main one, but you may also want an Instagram, LinkedIn, YouTube, Snapchat, Twitter, Pinterest, or blogging site profile to help create awareness about your business. Do not feel like you have to do them all, but at very least make a Facebook business profile.

3.– Citation listings will make it easier for people searching for your service to find your company. They also build your websites creditably with the search engines and they will in turn rank you higher and more often. This step should not be overlooked!

4.– Ask your customers for reviews. There are not many things that will shed better light on your company than having your customers vouch for you by posting reviews online. Remember, Google, Yelp, and Facebook are the 3 most beneficial places for someone to leave you a review.

5.– Determine your guarantee and display it on your website. Also consider putting it on some of your marketing pieces.

6.– Once you have the money available, invest in uniforms for yourself and your employees, along with graphics for your company vehicles.

7.– Yard signs are a great, inexpensive way to target customers for a specific service in a specific location. These also work very well for time specific services such as seeding and leaf removal!

8.– Consider paid ads online with Google, Bing, or Facebook or doing an EDDM campaign with the USPS. These types of ads get a little more expensive, but can provide a great return as well. Make sure you have the money to spend and the man- manpower to handle new work before doing any of these. It is also very important that the ads look very good and are very well written for these to be successful. It may be best to consult a professional for help.

CHAPTER 11

Customers

I had to pick which subject to go over next, customers or employees. I chose customers because if you can't find and keep customers, you are not going to need employees! That made that decision pretty easy. As you grow your business, how you handle your relationship with both is going to play a huge role in your success. I still believe the most important thing is that you do high-quality work at a fair price, and are reliable.

It is also critical to gain the respect of both your customers and employees. If your clients don't respect you they will not want to do business with you, and if your employees don't respect you they will not work for you, or worse, will do poor quality work for you. How do you gain their respect? Regarding your customers, start with being polite in your communications and do what you say you are going to do. If you say you will email or call them tomorrow, then do it. If you quote a price and you under bid the job, you may just want to make this a learning experience and quote the next job correctly instead of raising your quoted price. If you do underprice a recurring service like lawn mowing, it may be necessary to professionally communicate your error to the customer and let them know if you are to continue the service the future services will be 'X' dollars instead of your originally quoted price. It just comes down to being honest and reliable and doing high-quality work at a fair price over time. That works every time.

Gaining the respect of your employees is a little different. I feel the best way to do this is to be an expert at the services you offer and out work everyone on your crew. Be the first guy in and the last guy out. You should be doing that anyway if you are trying to grow your business. As your business grows, your role as the owner should also change. For example, I am not working in the field at all anymore. So, I am not physically outworking them, or staying later than them at this point. But, they know I can and would if needed, and they saw me do this for years before being able to do this. Your ethics will play a role in the amount of respect you get from both too, especially on the employee side because they will have closer interactions with you on a more frequent basis. How you conduct yourself inside and outside of work will affect how people treat you as the owner. You really need to consider the consequences of doing anything illegal or unethically when owning a company, although everyone should be doing this anyway. Let's focus on the customer aspect of your business now. We will cover employees in the next chapter.

Every business should determine their ideal customer. This is referred to as your demographic. It will affect decisions you make as you grow your business. Is your ideal client a residential property with under 10,000 square feet of turf or is it an industrial factory with 8 acres of turf? Either one could be a money maker for you, but you will need to purchase equipment and market appropriately to attract and efficiently service these different types of clients. Also, similar people tend to hang out together. If you can pick up a handful of your ideal clients and impress the hell out of them, they magically start referring you to their friends, family, neighbors, and co-workers.

Here is the most important thing to understand about customers. They provide the income that allows your business to operate. They pay you, your taxes, your employees, and for your equipment. Never forget that! You need to treat your customers like gold. I am not saying the customer is always right, but you should do your best to make them feel that way. Understand that if a client is not happy with your service you probably have failed to set proper expectations.

Make sure your customers reside your service area. When I got started, I was taking anyone and everyone who called my phone. This led to 20 and 30-minute drives between stops. Excessive drive time will kill your ability to make money. You lose money driving from stop to stop no matter what. You are burning gas, and the value of your vehicle is going down every mile. So, even if you aren't paying your guys while they are driving, because they are on a percentage pay system, this is still hurting you. If you are paying them by the hour, then this is killing you. Also, make sure your customers are ok with the limited number of services you offer. If they want a one stop shop for everything and you only mow and treat lawns like I do, then this customer is not the one for you. You will have to learn to say no! If you cannot develop this ability, there is a very good chance your business will not make enough profit to ever produce the money and freedom you had envisioned it would.

I have had the full gamut of clients over the years of running my business. I have had the best and the worst customers out there. When you get a good customer, they need to become a priority. On the other end of the spectrum, if you end up finding out that a client is not an ideal client, then it is time to cut ties. I know a lot of business owners have trouble dropping a problem customer. If you cannot make a client happy which is leading to multiple phone calls and emails, all of which eat away at you little by little, it's time to do something. The easiest thing to do is raise your prices. If the customer is not happy and you let them know you need to raise your prices to continue service, they will probably cancel service and solve this problem for you. Your attitude and mindset have to stay positive in this industry, and if someone, anyone, involved in your business is negative, they have got to go fast whether they are a customer, an employee, or a vendor.

Another reason to drop a customer is for non-payment. It is going to happen. I know a lot of guys who are like, "But if I stop cutting my lawn, they will never pay me!" Well, sorry to be frank, but they apparently aren't going to pay you anyway! Cut your losses and try to collect your money by using one of the methods described earlier.

Ask your customers how they prefer to communicate. Some people still prefer a phone call, while others would rather email or text. In my opinion, all of these methods are appropriate, and you should accommodate them. I highly prefer email as it leaves a trail of documents to reference if needed. Listen to your customers when they give you feedback. A lot of clients can be made happy by the simplest things such as a call ahead before service, or if you do a little extra like trim out the weeds growing in the cracks in their driveway. When they give you little hints like this, note their account so whoever goes to do that job knows to do these things. If their request is time-consuming, talk to your customer like a professional. Let them know you are happy to handle their additional request and explain what the additional cost per service would be. You are in business to make money. Never feel bad about charging a fair price for the specific services a client wants. They have other options and can get some other company to do the work if you are not a good fit. It will be better for everyone that way.

An excellent way to get feedback is by surveying your clients. When you send your invoices, ask them to complete a short survey. If you do this on a regular basis, you can make the surveys as short as a couple of questions. Shorter surveys will get you a better response rate. Try a service like SurveyMonkey to make this process super easy and very professional. Another thing you can do is incentivize your customers to participate in the survey by giving away a gift card. Maybe you give everyone who completes the survey a $5 Starbucks gift card, or maybe you could have a drawing for a $50 gift card to a local restaurant for anyone who completes the survey. People are busy these days. That very well may be the reason they are using your service in the first place. Make it worth their time because the information you receive could be priceless.

One last thing, put yourself in your customer's shoes. If you hired a company to mow your lawn, what would an excellent service entail? Here are some tips on how to stand out to your clients without spending much time or money. Do the little things such as take their newspaper from their driveway to their front porch or return the empty garbage cans to their storage location. Pick up any kids or dog toys before mowing and set them in a safe place. Pick up and dispose of any trash or debris that may be on the lawn. Then just provide a high-quality professional service. Don't be cussing at your mower because the blade won't engage for 10 seconds for some reason and don't do bonehead things like plaster their mulch beds or cars with grass. Maybe the property has weeds growing in the cracks in the drive, or they have little beds which you could weed in a couple of minutes. Do it! Do these small insignificant things because your competition is not and this will put your head and shoulders above them in the customer's eyes.

The best way to keep a positive and healthy relationship with your clients is by being very responsive to their phone calls, voicemails, and texts. Do not leave them hanging. Remember, they provide the income for your business to operate! Get back with your customers the same day they contact you if they contact you before business hours are over. Even if you can't answer their question, shoot them an email to let them know you received their message and you will get back with them tomorrow after you have time to look into it.

Chapter 11 – Action Steps

1.– Remember without your customers, you have no income! That is rule number 1!

2.– Determine your ideal client? Where do they live? How old are they? Do they have kids? How big is their lawn? Etc.

3.– Always be polite and professional with all communications.

4.– Answer the phone if at all possible. Remember you are running a business, it does not have to be you that personally answers the phone! If you can't answer, call them back as quick possible. Return emails promptly also.

5.– Drop problem customers like a bad habit.

6.– Determine the little extra things that don't cost much money, if any, and also take very little time to do, to really standout to your customers. This is what keeps them with you and gets them talking about you to their friends, family, and neighbors.

CHAPTER 12

Employees

Oh, employees… Employees are the critical factor in any lawn care or landscaping company that has the intention of growing and serving a lot of clients, which will allow you to make serious money. No one can argue that a company with ten employees has the potential to create more revenue that a company with two employees assuming they are providing similar services. This is leverage. Employees in a lawn care business are tools that allow the owner to leverage his or her time. Meaning, potentially the owner of the company could be sitting on a beach somewhere while his or her employees are completing jobs and generating income for the company, and subsequently the owner. I have employed over 100 people running my lawn care business, and this is from where I draw the information I will provide to you in this section.

I must admit I was not able to figure out a good way to attract quality employees. That is why I modified my business as time went on to make it work with the handful of good employees I was able to find. Once again, referencing Grant Cardone's book Be Obsessed or Be Average, Grant does not deny the lack of talent or motivation in the available unemployed pool of people in America. I like Grant because he keeps it real, if you will. But he goes on to say, that there are 7.3 billion people on earth right now and if you truly believe none of those people would be a great fit for your company, you are incorrect.

As soon as you go into business, you need to put your big boy pants on and take responsibility. Anything that goes wrong in your company is going to be your fault, whether you personally had anything to do with the specific mishap or not. If you can't handle it, you need to close shop or stay solo. After reading Grant's book, I reflected on my business and my struggles with finding employees over the years. I honestly asked myself if I had done everything I could have done to find the right employees, and the answer was a definite no. No, I did not. If I truly wanted to find that employee when I needed him, I would have been relentless letting everyone I know that I needed an employee. I would have blasted it out on social media, and yes, I would have done the unthinkable, I would have stopped every crew I saw out working for another company and asked them if they wanted to come to my company and make more money. I would have gotten the employee I needed if I did those three things every day until the employee appeared at my office ready to work.

Posting a job listing on ziprecruiter.com, indeed.com, or Craigslist are passive ways to attract an employee. You are not going to have much luck with this if any. People that are not employed do not have a job for a reason. Be extra cautious hiring someone that is not currently employed. People looking for a job on ziprecruiter.com or indeed.com probably want employment in an office setting or sales. People searching for a job on Craigslist are probably on crack. Let's be honest here people, the quality of the person you will find on Craigslist has great potential to not be a good fit for your business. I am making general assumptions, and that is not right. I am trying to get my point across. I personally responded to a Craigslist ad to get the job which lead to me starting my company. There are always exceptions to the rule, but there is also always the norm.

I hear this all the time, "Don't hire friends or family." Who the BLEEP started this garbage saying? In my experience, this could not be further from the truth. I now literally only employee friends and family in my business. You know what I need to worry about employing my friends and relatives? Just about nothing. When I hired Joe Blow, I needed to worry about everything, or at least I should have. I have had many employees I had never met until interviewing and hiring them. They seemed like decent people, then proceeded to do everything from steal from me to shoot heroin on one of my customer's properties. Some of these employees were great at performing the work. I had one guy tell me he came to work high for his week and a half and he thought that would be okay with me. Are you freaking serious? The largest theft by an employee cost me about $1700 to replace all the stolen equipment. If you have friends and family that are willing to work for you, hire them. Treat them like any other employee. Business is business, and that is that.

One thing I would like to interject regarding hiring employees is to not focus on their ability to perform the work. Ask anyone successful in business, and they will tell you to hire a person with integrity, a good attitude, and willingness to learn over skill any day. If you happen to find all these qualities in one person, hire them and treat them well. You will need to train any new hire to your way of doing business. This will be training them on the systems of your business. If you do hire someone with no experience, please know that it is going to be a long slow process to get them up to speed. How well you are able to train your employees will also play a huge role in your company's success, so you need to have a good training program. Experience is the best teacher. If possible, have your new hires go out on your crew or on one of your best crew leader's crew to learn the ropes. The employees that got to go out with me for a year or two are hands down the best employees I ever had. They did not only learn how to do each task involved in the job, but also how to work hard, efficiently, and professionally.

I can't stress enough how important it is to screen your employees before you hire them. Make them fill out an application. You need to have an application on file for every employee anyway. Call their previous employers and their references. This is a quick, easy way to eliminate people you don't want in your company. If someone lies on their application, do not hire them. If their references do not have tons of good things to say about them, do not hire them. I have called references that didn't even know the person that had applied to my company. I think they just made up name and number to put on the application thinking I would never call.

Before you hire anyone, you should have them sign their copy of your company's employee handbook. The employee handbook should lay out very clearly what is expected of the employee once hired. This includes everything from your dress code, appearance in regard to hair, facial hair, piercings, and tattoos, your call off policy, late policy, attitude, harassment, illegal activity, and more. Your handbook will come in very handy if you ever need to fire someone. If the employee clearly violated a policy in your handbook, you can then present this information to the unemployment division and you will not have to pay their unemployment. You should have your lawyer review your handbook or even draw it up for you. One thing to note about employee handbooks if you are going to implement this in your business and you already have employees, is that you will need to compensate them for signing it after their employment has begun. This could be a small bonus, a paid day off, or something along those lines.

You should also have job descriptions for your employees. This will outline their role and responsibilities in your company. You will want to have job descriptions for each position in your company, and it is not a bad idea to include yourself in this as well. As you develop employees, you can delegate some of your tasks to your employees as they get more comfortable with their current responsibilities. This will free up your time to concentrate on growing your business, making it more efficient, and communicating with your customers. It is smart to include, and whatever is asked of you, as part of your job description as roles and responsibilities may change over time.

Sorry I could not be more help on finding employees, but I do know how to retain employees once you get them! I have never been big on job titles. I don't like my employees calling me their boss, although they do on a regular basis. I prefer the team atmosphere. I need everyone on my team working towards a common goal which is always satisfied customers. Since we are a business, we need to create these satisfied customers in an efficient manner which allows the company to profit. The more the company profits, the better I can compensate my employees.

So, most important is making the employees feel like they play a significant role in your business. This really shouldn't be that hard to do. Treat everyone fairly and always compliment your crew any and every chance you get. If a customer emails and says the crew did a good job, forward the email to them. If they call in and tell you, shoot your crew leader a text and tell him to tell the rest of the crew. When I get a new guy on one of my mowing crews, and he is starting off as the trimmer and blower, I tell them this, "Our lawn mowing service consists of three parts: Mowing, edging/trimming, and blowing. They are all equally important. We will get you comfortable on a mower as fast as we can, but for these jobs to be successful right now, we still need all three aspects of the job completed professionally. If a single part is not done correctly, the whole service is going to be a failure. I need you to concentrate and get proficient at all three aspects so we can continue to impress our customers with every service we perform. The first aspect to master is trimming and edging."

Employees definitely want to feel important. Make sure you make them feel this way as often as possible. I am going to take a wild guess here and assume they also want to earn money. I encourage you to pay your employees as well as you can. They need to be compensated in direct proportion to the value they provide to your company. If you hire a 19-year-old kid with no experience, you will need to start him out on the low end of the pay scale as he is providing minimal value to your company. He just has potential which he can live up to, or not. If you have an experienced crew leader who can take this 19-year-old kid out with him and cut twenty $50 properties a day flawlessly, he needs to be compensated in direct portion to that. Never forget that some people are motivated by things other than money. In lawn care, this seems to be a paid day off, or even just a day off without pay. Work a couple paid days off for each of your guys into your pricing. Holidays that happen to be occur during the work week are a great example of a time to offer your guys a paid day off.

Up until this past season, I paid my employees by the hour. I usually started guys at $10 an hour until they started learning the ropes. I would let them know, once you can do this, whether it be trim properly or edge professionally or use the mower, let me know, and I will come check you out. When you can weed eat professionally, I can pay you $11 an hour and so on, for the different milestones. My crew leaders were making between $16 and $17 per hour, and they were getting around 55 hours per week. A lot of the time they would gross over $1k per week, but they were also getting burned out with this workload. They couldn't see the potential to make more money because they had no desire to work more hours in a week. I couldn't blame them, but on the other hand, myself as the owner of the company often put in 80 plus hours in a week. When my business was ramping up, I often didn't pay myself for months at a time. I was reinvesting everything back into my business to build a bigger and brighter future. It paid off for me.

Now I pay my guys on a percentage pay system. Some people call this piecework, piece pay, or performance pay. This method of paying employees is prevalent in other industries and is legal. I can't tell you how many people want to tell me that this is illegal or that I am cheap and treat my employees like garbage because I pay them like this. I don't understand. Talk to my employees and ask them how they like the percentage pay system. They freaking love it. The only thing you need to be careful with on a percentage pay system is minimum wage. Although this should never be an issue, you must still track each employee's hours every week to make sure they at least made minimum wage including overtime if applicable. My guys blow their hourly wage pay out of the water with their percentage pay. My most experienced mowing crew members make $1k gross almost every week and work an average of 43 hours per week. Our season lasts about 39 weeks from start to finish. At $1k a week they are making $39k per year, but remember they still have 13 weeks to make more money some other way. They could and should be making money when they aren't at work during the working season. I couldn't imagine only having one source of income. Think about how you can create a separate stream of income to complement your lawn care or landscaping business.

I am a huge fan of the percentage pay system because it compensates your employees when they produce revenue for your company. No more getting paid to stop at the gas station for snacks or for taking the long route to the next job! If you decide to implement a percentage pay system prepare to watch productivity go up. I can't tell you exactly what your percentage pay rate should be. This is going to directly correlate to your pricing, company's overhead, variable expenses, and revenue it generates. If you have existing numbers to work with, play around with different percentages to find what percentage correlates to what their hourly pay currently is. That would be a great starting point. Learn more about percentage pay at LawnCrack.com in the resources section.

Another reason I like performance pay is that you will now know your labor cost to perform each job. You no longer need to worry about your employees taking an extra five minutes on every job. On the hourly pay system, these extra five minutes on each job end up being thousands of dollars paid to your employees over the course of a season. Assuming you know your overhead and have a good grasp on the variable expenses to complete the various jobs, you will know your profit as well. My guys know all I care about is that the work gets done on schedule and done right. If the work is not done right, they understand they are responsible for going back and making it right with the customer. They also know there is no additional pay for doing this. They know they are expected to do the job right the first time and have already been compensated. I will be out a little gas money and some wear and tear on my equipment, but that is all.

I can't stress enough how critical finding and retaining quality employees will be if your goal is to own a business. Without them, you as the owner, are left to handle all of the responsibilities, and once again, this is owning a job. You have to understand that you will rarely find an employee that cares as much or completes jobs at the same pace and quality level as you do. You cannot let them know you are upset with them because of this. As the owner, you need to keep a cool, level head when in the presence of your employees. Do anything you can to encourage them to get better and faster at their job. The percentage pay system is a great way to accomplish this.

Employees are not wired the same way as business owners. They do not feel the same level of responsibility as we do. If at all possible, try to safeguard against employees leaving you high and dry. Employees will call in from time to time, even the best of them. You will need to make sure your company is still able to complete the workload each week even if short staffed. Once you are able to get yourself out of the field, you should be able to jump in and run a crew or route solo if needed due to employees not showing up for work to cover them and keep everything on track.

Until you get to the point where you have five crews out each day, I would not even consider hiring an office person. I have had three office employees over the years, one at a time. I can now confidently tell you I will never hire an office person again for my lawn care company. If you do, I would strongly suggest setting up a secret camera in your office so you can monitor what they are doing all day. I know for a fact I paid my office people for many hours of them surfing the web and making personal purchases online while on my clock. You can outsource the answering of your business phone to some type of call center so you are not distracted by the incoming calls all day. I would recommend looking into that as an alternative to hiring an inhouse office person to answer your phone. Maybe your mom, grandma, girlfriend, or wife would do it for free. Think outside the box and focus on making more money and spending less to do it!

Chapter 12 – Action Steps

1.– Start looking for employees before you need them!

2.– Call all references before hiring anyone.

3.– You will need to develop a training system to get new guys up to speed. The best way I have found to develop a great employee is take them with you on your crew or one of your best crew leader's crew for 6, 12, or 18 months, however long it takes.

4.– Have every employee sign an employee handbook before they get hired.

5.– Create job descriptions for each position. Always include, 'and whatever is asked of you,' as part of the job description!

6.– Make your employees feel important and appreciated.

7.– Consider paying employees on a percentage pay system. Get more info at LawnCrack.com/resources

CHAPTER 13

Services to Offer

So far, I have only used lawn mowing as the service offered. I did that to keep things straightforward and easy to understand. I also think it is a good idea only to provide lawn mowing while you are getting started and building a customer base. Lawn mowing often leads to the client asking you to perform other lawn and landscape type services. It is easier to upsell a current customer than it is to pick up a new client and it is less expensive that way!

I will list out several other lawn and landscape type services and add my two cents for each. I am sure I will not include them all. The important thing here is to not over extend yourself. You can only do so much. As your team grows and you hire new talent, it may open the doors to offering other services in the future. Don't rush into providing all these services. I will go into more detail on offering a mowing service before I get into the other services.

I used to use the old-fashioned truck and trailer method to haul around my lawn mowers. I now use modified box trucks I purchased used from U-Haul. All we did was slap our logos on them and had folding gates fabricated on the back. It was one of the best decisions I ever made and here are the reasons why. All of my equipment is covered and protected when not in use. This is nice when it starts raining and the crew still needs to travel back to our shop, but it is excellent because we can still shut the back door and lock it once the truck returns. This eliminated my rent expense because I no longer needed a storage location for my equipment. My employees take the trucks back to their homes and if they have a crew member, the crew member starts and stops each day from their crew leader's house. I bought them the stuff need to maintain the mowers and they pull them into their garage and do any maintenance there too. My crew leaders love it because they have zero drive time to and from work as an additional bonus. Obviously, you need trustworthy employees to be able to do this.

As I stated earlier, I am not going to tell you which brand of mower or trimmer to buy, but I recommend making sure you have a local dealer nearby for whichever brand you choose to go with. Buy the appropriate deck size and mower type for your client base or the client base you are going after. Each of my mowing trucks has a 61" zero turn, a 48" walk behind, and a 30" push mower. We run 48" walk behinds instead of 52" walk behinds because there is little productively loss since the deck is only 4" narrower, but you would be surprised how many more gates a 48" can fit in compared to a 52". I used to run 36" walk behinds to get in the smaller gates, but I now use 30" oversized push mowers for this task. The reason being a 30" mower costs about a 1/3 of the price as a 36" walk behind hydro and we rarely need to use them anyway. I would encourage you to spend the extra few dollars and buy a hydro drive mower over a belt drive for greater safety, more functionality, and increased productivity. If you have hills in your area, a walk behind is going to make more sense than a stand on or zero turn mower. When you can only afford one or two mowers as you are getting started, make sure you can use them on the majority of properties in your area.

As far as string trimmers and blowers go, I recommend going with the middle of the line professional grade of whichever brand you prefer. Unless your business has an unusual need for all the power of the top of the line models, these mid-grade models will be able to get the job done professionally, usually weigh less, and burn less fuel. I don't know why anyone would pick a handheld blower over a backpack blower. As soon as I could afford a backpack blower, I started only purchasing those and never looked back. Regarding the string trimmer, you will want a straight shaft over a curved shaft and run .105 trimmer line instead of a smaller diameter line. The difference in cut quality and speed is vast. I have never used a stick edger and see no reason to ever use one. In my opinion, using a dedicated stick edger to edge your concrete borders is a complete waste of time as the string trimmer can do it just as well with a properly trained operator and then you can just continue on trimming the rest of the lawn without having to switch pieces of equipment. I do understand it is easier to train someone to properly use a stick edger, it throws less debris out, and there may be some other benefits in certain situations. I think this just comes down to your preference, but know stick edging will add time to the jobs and be another expense.

Fertilization and weed control is one of the odd ball services in my opinion. What I mean by this is that you need to be certified to perform this service and many companies that offer fertilization and weed control, only offer that service, or they may also offer aerations and seeding services to compliment it. My company provided this service from the beginning because I was certified and had worked for the largest lawn treatment company in the United States a few short years before starting my company. Getting certified is not very hard. You will need to contact your state's Department of Agriculture, get the study material, and then pass the test. If you are going to offer this service, you should have a passion for it and know a lot about turf health, diseases, weeds, best practices, etc. It only makes sense. This is an aggravating service to provide because it seems no matter what you do the weeds continually re-enter the lawn. You can keep weeds to a minimum, but it is challenging to keep a lawn entirely weed free. It is a non-stop losing battle unless the customer is willing to invest in overseeding to thicken up their turf and crowd out the weeds. Weeds are such an issue because they can survive and even thrive, in deplorable soil conditions and with little water.

You can get away with providing lawn treatment services with a push spreader and handheld sprayers to spray the weeds. This would be the cheap, quick way to start offering this service. If you are going to do this at scale, you will probably want to invest in a skid sprayer that would go in the back of one of your trucks or get a ride on sprayer/spreader which are becoming more and more popular these days. If you are going to make this into a real revenue generator for your company, you will want to dedicate a truck to this service. We use a skid sprayer in combination with an Eco-505 unit from Gregson Clark. The Eco-505 saves us thousands of dollars on weed control each year, not to mention how much it reduces the amount of chemicals we unnecessarily introduce into the environment. I recommend you consider the Eco-505 if you are using a skid sprayer. They can be added to almost any existing unit.

If you do want to get into treating lawns, think of how you can separate your service from the others in your area. We did this by offering a hybrid organic program. The fertilization aspect of our program is completely organic. We brew compost tea that goes directly into the spray tanks before the truck goes out each morning. Not only does this reduce our product cost, but it also is very beneficial to the soil. More and more people are becoming concerned with the environment. Going the organic route is a great way to pick up some clients from company's still running all synthetic programs. With the volume of lawns we treat, I have not been able to find an effective organic weed control. That is why we call it hybrid organic, because the weed control portion is still synthetic. I do make sure our customers know we have the Eco-505 which greatly reduces the amount of herbicide we apply to their lawn though.

Overseeding services is another option you can easily offer. The most common way this service is performed is by doing an aeration and overseed. We will also touch on slice seeding and dethatching briefly. You could buy the equipment you need to carry out these services as my company did, or you could rent them when you need them. Keep in mind that all the other companies will be seeding at the same time as you during the season which may make renting this equipment hard or impossible. That is why I just bought reliable used machines. I also feel like the time it takes to pick up and drop off rental equipment eats into your profit pretty quickly. Check with your local Home Depot's tool rental department and ask if they have any equipment for sale. I got a very lightly used Classen slice seeder and dethatcher from them for cheap! Keep in mind, the tool rental department is in the business of renting tools. You can work them down on the asking price. The same applies if you go to buy a used U-Haul truck from U-Haul.

If you plan on offering aerations as a service, please make sure you are using a core aerator. Spike type aerators do more harm than good in most cases. Dethatching is beneficial when the thatch layer builds up too thick on the soil surface. Not too many companies offer this service, so it may be a niche you can take over in your market. Slice seeding is very similar to dethatching and may yield better results that aerating and overseeding in particular situations. Make sure you are using the appropriate type of grass seed and put it down at the right rate. Like any other service you offer, make sure you have a solid understanding of how to properly do it. You don't want to offer any service in which you are not confident that the finished product is going to look great. You also need to make sure you have an accurate estimation of material costs and time involved in the job. The reason I mention this here is that if you don't have a good system to pick up the thatch after detatching, you could quickly find yourself losing money on the job.

My biggest issue with offering seeding services is that you rely on the homeowner to water to have a successful service. Make sure you educate them on proper watering practices! We ended up having to redo many seeding jobs for free to make the customer happy, but I honestly think the only part of the service that went wrong was the watering portion. To me, it was worth it to lose a little money or break even by redoing parts of the job to keep the customer happy. I would then re-emphasize the importance of watering, so they didn't make the same mistake again. Last note on seeding services is that they primarily occur in the spring and fall, so if you are booked up with your primary season long services, you may not have the time or man power to work these jobs in when they need to be done.

Some of the most common landscape maintenance services include spring and fall clean ups, mulching, pruning, and leaf removals. My first bit of advice here is not to do any of these services if you don't have a cheap and convenient place to get mulch and to dispose of debris. It is hard to make money and charge a fair price if you do not have these two things available to you. Ideally, you would have bulk mulch with a machine to load it and a burn pile or compost pile at your business location. This set up is going to cost a decent amount of money in most areas. Not to say you cannot make money without these two things as I certainly have in the past, but you are limiting your profitably if are not set up properly.

To perform this type of work you will need to invest in a whole array of additional equipment. You will need to get everything from rakes and shovels to chain saws and hedge trimmers, to wheel barrows and dump trailers. While you don't need a dump truck or dump trailer, keep in mind time is money and labor is labor. If you are going to be in business, you must have the equipment necessary to provide these services. If you don't, it is doubtful offering these services is contributing to your bottom line. I just listed some tools you may need, but also think about the amount of space of these tools will take up. The cheaper your location is to operate means less of your income is going to overhead expenses. If you can operate out of a smaller square foot building, typically your cost will go down. Naturally, being able to offer these services increases your ability to create more revenue, but I want to you consider the pros and cons. Everything reaches a point of diminishing returns. I learned this the hard way and want to save you the time, money, and aggravation. I highly encourage you to niche your business down. My company now only offers mowing and lawn treatment services. Previously we were a full-service lawn, landscape, hardscape, and snow removal company. Once I limited the number of services I offered to two, I saw my profit increase tremendously.

Getting a little deeper into landscaping, you have landscape design and installation. Providing design and install services can quickly lead to landscape lighting, ponds, irrigation, and hardscapes. To provide these services, you must have expertise in these areas. I honestly think most lawn care companies have no business offering these services. You should only provide these services if you are a true expert. You can certainly get away with throwing in some plants here and there, but you are doing your customer a disservice by offering to provide these services when you are not entirely competent. So, if you are, then knock yourself out. You will really shine providing these services among the wannabes. I am not going to get into the details of these services because if you do want to offer these services, you should already know how to do them and what you will need to do them.

The services I covered so far are the core of the industry. There are all kinds of add on services and seasonal services that can complement this core offering and create additional revenue for your company in the process. Some things to think about are annual flower installation, perimeter pest control, mole control, bed maintenance, and pressure washing. There are lots of other odd ball services you could throw in here too. I still encourage you to stick with your core service or two and run with those. Become the very best in your area at those services and charge a premium. I am using lawn mowing as the core service in this book, but maybe your core service is landscape maintenance instead. It doesn't matter which service you pick. The point is to keep it manageable. Everything will be simpler, and profit margins will be greater. I am not saying to charge an unfair amount for the services you excel in, but charge according to the value you can provide your clients.

Another reason my company only offers a lawn mowing service and a lawn treatment service is that they both create recurring revenue. This creates stability in my business. We mow each lawn approximately 30 times in a season and we run a 6-step treatment program. Therefore, we have cash flowing into the company throughout the season. Often mulching is a 1-time service each season. Pruning is typically done twice in a season, or possibly 3 or 4 times when you get those customers who are fanatics about their lawn and landscape. I always liked that kind of customer as long as they were reasonable! A lot of the other services are similar to mulching and pruning. I hope you can see the greater revenue potential and greater stability offered by recurring services over every now and then services.

An additional service related to our industry is tree removal. The most successful tree removal companies I see are dedicated tree service companies. All they do is cut down trees and grind stumps. It is funny that it almost seems like they are taking my advice on focusing on 1 or 2 services, becoming proficient at them, and charging a premium! Wow. Word of caution, if you are not a tree service and insist on doing tree work, you will want to double check with your insurance provider. More than likely your lawn and landscape general liability insurance policy does not provide coverage if you drop a tree on someone's house. Even the insurance agencies know these are separate services and should be treated as such.

Wrapping up the service section is snow removal. I really can't pick out words to describe just how much I hate snow removal. At my company's largest point, we had four snow trucks out each storm. I know snow removal is a much more significant service in some parts of the country and is not a service at all in other regions. With my company located just south of Cincinnati, we were right in the hit or miss zone. One year we would remove $75k worth of snow and the next $0. That is not the only reason why I hate snow removal. The hours are terrible and unpredictable, and did I mention it is always freezing when it snows. Yeah…Well, it is. I highly encourage you not to do snow removal no matter how cool you think it is or because "I can charge $100 per hour to plow." By the time all the trucks were repaired from the wear and tear of plowing and hauling thousands of pounds of salt around, I honestly bet I never made a dollar plowing snow or spreading salt. You don't have to waste all this time and money. Please just learn from my mistakes! If you have the financial ability to get through the winter without making any money, use this time to improve your business.

Chapter 13 – Action Steps

1.– Really put some thought into the services you offer. Are you really good at all of them? Do some services require overhead expenses that are not justified? Are you having trouble finding employees able to do a certain service? Are one or two services you offer forcing you to stay in a more expensive shop to house the equipment? Do you enjoy offering every service? List your services in order based off how profitable they are and consider the other factors mentioned to determine if you should be offering all of those services or not.

CHAPTER 14

Business Finances

This book wouldn't be complete without diving into the financial portion of running a business. The success of your business will ultimately come down to how well you manage your finances. This does cross over into your personal finances as well as poor decisions with your personal finances can and will negatively affect your business. K-12 schools do not teach people about making money, managing money, or investing money. The lack of financial education is evidenced by the poor financial state most people find themselves in today. You do not have to be one of them! In this section, I will cover: income and expenses, taxes, man hour rates, pricing your services, and large purchases.

It is critical that your business takes in more income than it costs you to produce that income at all stages of your business. Tech start up these days operate at a loss until they reach their critical number of users to start showing a profit, or they go belly up trying to gain the market share they need to survive. I am assuming you do not have the luxury of being backed by venture capital. Not to worry though, I made this work in my business, and you can do the same.

Your income will primarily be generated by payments from clients if it is not the sole source of your business' income. Maybe you have a year or two of past numbers to reference to get an estimate of what you can expect your business to produce next year and the associated costs. If not, you can use the Profitability Calculator at LawnCrack. com to estimate how many jobs your company can do and the amount of money you can expect to earn over the course of one year. Once you have an idea of what kind of money you can expect to bring in, we will look at costs associated with running your business to be able to generate that revenue. Our Profitability Calculator is like a plug and play profit and loss statement. It is free in the resource section at LawnCrack.com.

Expenses can be broken down into overhead expenses and variable expenses. Your overhead expenses are going to remain the same from month to month or year to year, while variable costs will be affected by hours worked and amount of use among other things. Examples of overhead expenses include rent, truck payments, and insurance. Overhead expenses are also referred to as fixed costs or operating expenses. Examples of variable expenses include most wages, gas, and materials. Variable costs are also referred to as Cost of Goods Sold or COGS. An easy way to determine what is an overhead expense versus a variable expense is by asking yourself if you stopped performing any work, and therefore had no variable costs, what expenses would remain? These are your overhead expenses. A quick note regarding wages as relating to overhead or variable costs. The owner's salary, sales people, and office staff could be an overhead expense, but your employees out in the field completing the work will always be a variable expense.

One thing that will help is if you start thinking like a bottom line guy instead of a top line guy. Not that I want to limit you in any way as to how much revenue your business brings in, the top line, but what is more important is the bottom line. The bottom line is how much profit is left after all expenses have been paid. Let's look at this quick example to make sure you understand what I mean. If two businesses both have $200k in revenue, but it cost one company $180k to bring in that $200k and it took the other company $130k, you can see there is a big difference. In this case, there is a $50k difference. That $50k is profit that flows right down to the owner of the company. You can become more profitable by making the same amount of money and spending less to make it. It took me a long time to realize this. Please closely look at every dollar leaving your company and first determine if it is a necessary expense. If it is, is there a cheaper alternative?

A general good rule of thumb is to minimize your expenses as much as possible. You can do this in many ways, and I don't want you buying cheap or old equipment to make this happen. Shopping and comparing insurance rates is an excellent example of a way many companies could lower their overhead. Financing equipment is a great way to get a piece of equipment that you cannot afford to pay for outright. Maybe you don't have $6k to spend on a new walk behind mower, but can you make the $125 payment for the next 48 months? I would hope you can or will be able to soon after reading this book. Debt is not bad in business. If used properly it is a form of leverage, and a means to make more money more efficiently. Can you purchase items in bulk to lower the price per piece or can you find the part you need on the internet instead of buying it at the local dealer for twice as much? Can you get all of your work done in four 10-hour days instead of five 8-hour days? These are just a few ways to lower your expenses, and there are many more possibilities out there.

The largest expenses you will have in a lawn and landscape business are wages, rent, insurance, and gas, and possibly vehicles or large equipment depending on what exactly your business does. Focusing on these expenditures can yield the most substantial savings with the least amount of time and energy involved to do so. Can you pay your employees based on the revenue they produce instead of an hourly wage? Can you operate out of a smaller shop? Maybe you could run it out of your house, or out of a storage unit. Shop and compare insurance quotes from different carriers and be sure to see how different deductible limits affect your monthly payments. Have your crews check the GasBuddy app for the lowest gas prices. Sometimes there is a 30 to 50 cent difference in the price per gallon from gas stations located within a mile or two of each other. The savings can add up over the course of the year, or if not monitored, can lead to potential profit never making it to your bottom line.

You have to pay great attention to the money entering and exiting your business. This is a perfect example of the Peter Drucker quote, 'What gets measured gets improved.' You need to measure and compare the numbers on your profit and loss statement in order for you to know where changes need to be made. I don't want you to be cheap in business, because you will have to spend money to make money in this industry, but I do want you to be frugal. Do not get caught up in name brands and who has the biggest, newest, nicest truck. These things matter little to the profitability of your business. If the 3-year-old model of the truck you want will get the job done and costs $20k less than the new model, buy the used truck and keep your $20k.

Let's touch on taxes as they could be a significant expense also. One reason you should work with an accountant from the beginning is that they can help you better understand the tax liability of your business and ultimately save you money in the long run. I will provide some basic knowledge here. You have probably heard the saying, "It's a tax write off." Almost any legitimate expense of running your business can be written off your taxes. You can potentially lower your business' tax liability down to zero. If you had to spend $100k to make $100k, your tax liability could be zero. Now you're thinking, that is great, I can lower my tax liability to zero, but I don't make any money, so what's the point.

What you need to know is, using the $100k in revenue and $100k in expenses example, the owner of this company could have made $60k or more. If it is a solo operation using an LLC as the business entity and he choose to be taxed as an S-Corp, the owner could have paid himself $60k, and the business had $40k in other overhead and variable expenses, making the tax liability of the business zero. Depreciation can also skew the numbers on paper. Even though the business is not taxed, the owner would be taxed on the $60k in wages and distributions. You need to be careful doing this though. If your business is not showing a profit, the IRS can deem it as a hobby. You do not want to walk this line. Research the current IRS codes and consult with your CPA if you are trying to limit your tax liability to extremes like this. One side note on CPA's, if they say you should buy a piece of equipment or spend some money right before the year end to lower your tax liability, I would say RUN! In rare cases, this may be good advice, but it tells me your accountant does not know much about running a profitable business. Spending a dollar to save a dime is a loser's game to me. Although, if you legitimately need to purchase a piece of equipment, it could be a good financial decision.

This limiting of your tax liability is at the federal and state level. When you get down to the cities and counties, they will be taxing your business based on the revenue your company produces in their locality regardless of your expenses. These taxes are usually nominal percentages of the income you generate in their district, and often they will have a minimum charge to do business each year ranging from $10 to $300 or so in my experience. It is the cost of doing business. You will need to track what locality your income is being generated in. That is just another reason you should have a software program like Service Autopilot to help run your business. Once your business is up and running the IRS will probably make you start paying estimated tax payments on a quarterly basis throughout the year based on your prior year's earnings.

The last tax I want to touch on is payroll taxes. Over the years, I have had different payroll companies handle this differently. Payroll taxes will more than likely need to be submitted on a monthly or quarterly basis. I prefer for the payroll company to draw the amount due for taxes from my bank account each time payroll run occurs, but I have had some that did not take the money from my account and then hit me with a $6k payroll tax liability bill at the end of the quarter. I never had an issue with this as I manage money very well, but I can see how some people could get themselves into a lot of trouble very quickly.

My final advice on taxes is that the way you earn your income will determine how that income is taxed. I am not sure how well know of a fact this is, but it can make a big difference in your tax liability. Earned income is taxed at whatever rate is applicable to your tax bracket. Earned income is going to be the money you receive from your paycheck. If you are taxed as an S-Corp, the owner is also allowed to take distributions along with their wages. The distributions will be taxed at a lower rate. You will need to discuss this with your CPA, as the government expects you to pay yourself a 'reasonable salary' for the position you hold in your company. The easiest way to determine a reasonable salary is to pay yourself the same amount you would need to pay someone else to hold that position in your company. Anything you earn over that could then be paid as a distribution and taxed at a lower rate. The profits from the sale of a piece of equipment or your entire business would be a capital gain, and is taxed at a different rate than earned income or distributions. It gets a little confusing and is another reason to find a high-quality CPA.

These are the types of things many business owners never consider, especially in our industry. This really opens the door up for those willing to seek out the knowledge and implement it to their advantage. The green movement is another opportunity for tax savings. Many local and federal governments are offering tax incentives for solar, battery, and propane powered equipment. This could not only save you some tax dollars, but could also separate your company from those still solely relying on gas powered equipment. There is a growing population of customers that would prefer to use a green company, even if it means paying a little more for the service.

Chapter 14 – Action Steps

1.– Can any expenses be eliminated or reduced?
2.– Can you buy in bulk or online for cheaper pricing?
3.– Shop insurance every now and then and note the difference in cost by using different deductibles.
4.– Discuss how different types of income are taxed with your CPA.

CHAPTER **15**

Pricing Services

Nobody likes a low-baller! I hate low-ballers as they are somewhat ruining our industry whether they know it or not, and whether you want to admit it or not. People these days are cheap or broke, but either way, they want to pay as little as possible to get anything done. Here is my view on what low-ballers are doing. They think they are providing a service at a great price to the customer, but don't know their numbers at all, and are breaking even or possibly losing money with every underpriced service they provide. The customers get used to these low prices and don't want to pay a legitimate company a fair rate anymore. The low-ballers keep doing their thing until they run out of money and are forced to go out of business, but the customer still only wants to pay $25 to get their lawn mowed. This is why low-balling is such an issue to me. These low-ball companies simply do not know or understand their numbers or the effect they have on the lawn care industry.

Lawn and landscape is a service based industry, but we also have material costs for items such as mulch and plants, etc. So, how you price your service comes down to how much money you need to generate per man hour. A man hour is one hour of one person working. If three guys are on the job for one hour, that job took 3-man hours. You must understand this concept to be successful. It very simply comes down to knowing your numbers.

The specific numbers you need to know are your overhead expenses, variable expenses, and how many man hours will be worked. I recommend you break this down for each service you offer especially if specific pieces of equipment are used only for certain type jobs or if your wages vary considerably from crew to crew. Let's look at an example.

In this example, we will have an employee who makes $13 per hour and the company only mows grass. He is the only employee and does all of the work. The owner is hands off in this business and collects a little passive income each year from owning the business. In my area, the work year is roughly 39 weeks long. We need to multiply the wages of $13 per hour by 1.3 to account for payroll taxes and workers comp. We will also assume he worked 40 hours per week. So, $13 times 1.3 equals $16.90 actual cost per hour to employ this employee. $16.9 times 40 hours in a week equals $676 per week total cost, times 39 work weeks equals $26,364 for the season. There are 1560 total hours worked using these numbers.

Along with our wage expense, we will also have a $150 per month mower payment, $150 per month storage unit cost, and $150 per month insurance cost. These three overhead costs come to $5400 per year. We will estimate $3,500 for gas and maintenance expenses. And lastly, well use $2400 for phone and internet, and hopefully, any other miscellaneous expenses are accounted for within these numbers. The total expenditures to run this little business is $37,664.00. Now, all we need do is divide the total expenses by the hours worked, and we get $24.14. So, if everything goes as planned and no additional costs are incurred to operate this business, if $24.14 is generated for every hour the employee works, the business will break even. I don't know anyone who wants to run a company that breaks even. It seems like a lot of trouble to go through for nothing!

What if the business charged $40 per man hour instead of $24.14? Well, let's take $40 per man hour times the same 1560 hours, and we get $62,400. $62,400 minus our total costs of $37,664 equals $24,736. Remember that this number is gross and everything that can be written off has been already, so plan on roughly 30% of the gross to go to the government in the form of taxes. If we do that math, the owner of the company will net profit $17,315.20 when all is said and done, if he charges $40 per man hour. Not bad for a completely hands-off business.

Hopefully, now you can see why I can't just say you need to charge 'X' number of dollars per man hour. It is impossible for me to know without knowing your numbers. With that said, I believe most mowing services and lawn treatment services will be right around the $35 to $50 per man hour mark. When you get into landscaping and hardscaping, that man hour rate can go up significantly. You took the time to learn the lawn and landscape industry, took the risk of starting your business, and continued to learn and grow a business that provides a needed service to your community. There is no reason to be ashamed in any way if you prosper from your efforts.

Some more advice on pricing includes accounting for drive time, maintenance time, and shop time. Let's say you have a lawn that takes one guy 45 minutes to cut. The price of this job should include drive time to or from the next job, along with an extra minute or two to account for keeping the blades sharp and other maintenance tasks required to be able to perform the service. Always have a minimum charge for each service. One way to explode your income per hour is to perform a lot of minimum charge jobs. These jobs typically go super quick, and you end up getting more than your needed man hour rate.

I have had customers ask my why we need to charge $45, or whatever their price was, to perform the service when it only took us 10 or 15 minutes to complete the job. The fact of the matter is that we are able to complete the job in 10 to 15 minutes because we have purchased 10's of thousands of dollars' worth of equipment to be able to do so. We also do this professionally all day long, so we should be able to do it quickly. My favorite thing to say to this is, "How long did it take you to complete the job when you did it yourself?" The answer is usually an hour and a half or so, and they didn't even do the job to our quality standards. I then remind them of the cost of the equipment, maintenance, and gas when they did it themselves. Sometimes with the right client I would also bring up the opportunity cost of them performing the service themselves too. If you can politely and professionally put this in perceptive for them, it usually does the trick and they are happy to pay your price.

I wanted to expand on opportunity cost very quickly. Opportunity cost is what you stand to lose by choosing to one thing over another. This is why I want you to think before you choose to offer 8 different services and never get really profitable at any of them. The time you are spending fixing jobs, getting materials, and buying tools you now need, could have been spent perfecting how to become super profitable offering the one service you are best suited to offer. Trying to be the one stop shop almost put me out of business and I still see it happening to other companies in my area every day. Please do not fall into this trap!

The pricing section wouldn't be complete without discussing marking up material. I am a fan of the 20% markup in most situations. I also always account for wages or other expenses incurred while getting the materials too. To give you an example of what I mean let's look at getting plants from the nursery as an example. If it is a decent size install, I may be at the nursery for an hour picking out the plants. I will charge the customer for 1.5-man hours plus the cost of the plants multiplied by 20%. I added .5 hours to account for my drive time. I don't work for free and you shouldn't either. Some landscapers charge two times the cost of the plant or even three times. This makes zero sense. Don't do it. Charge accordingly for your time and materials. If you want to upsell the customer a warranty on the plants, that is up to you and has nothing do to with your price to install the plants.

It comes down to cash flow at the end of the day. As long as you have enough money available to pay your expenses when they are due, you are going to be okay. For the past couple years, I have acted like having $20k in my business bank account is like having $0 in my bank account. Once you figure out all the little intricacies of your business, you will have this luxury too. I hope the information in this book helps! I do this as a safety net. If you are in business long enough there will come a day where you need cash fast to make a necessary purchase to keep your business operating. This ties back in to being financial responsibility with your personal money. If you had taken that $20k and put a down payment on a car you couldn't afford or bought a boat, you would then be out of business when the crisis occurred, and you didn't have to cash to stay afloat.

I wish I had this book when I got started. I did read a similar how to start a lawn care business book, but it did not go into this much depth. If you still have questions, please reach out to us at LawnCrack.com. We also have our podcast titled Lawn Care Business Academy and the LawnCrack YouTube channel where you can learn valuable information to help your business become more profitable and consume less of your time.

Chapter 15 – Action Steps

1.– Find your break-even man hour rate. This is simply the grand total of expenses divided by hours worked for that same time frame. If you have material costs, these should be subtracted from your expense total before dividing by total man hours worked.

2.– After finding your break-even man hour rate…How much profit would you like to make? Say you want to profit $10,000 and you had 2,000 hours worked. You would need to charge $5 over your break-even man hour rate to achieve this.

3.– Establish a minimum charge for each service. Minimum charge jobs are often the most profitable.

CHAPTER 16

Purchasing Equipment

I wanted to touch on larger equipment purchases briefly. I am referring to items such as trucks, mowers, skid steers, and the like. Due to the high cost of these items, you may need to finance them instead of paying for them in full up front. Anytime you consider financing a piece of equipment ask yourself if it will produce more revenue than its cost per month, every month. If it does, it is more than likely a good purchase. If it doesn't, this is a piece of equipment that may be better to rent for the time being or you need to find a cheaper alternative.

If we go back to our walk behind mower purchase which cost $6k and was financed with 0% interest for 48 months, we get $125 per month as our monthly payment. We do need to factor in that we are only able to use the mower nine months out of the year. So, during the nine working months, it will need to produce $166.67 in revenue to cover its payments for the year. One person can cut $400 to $500, or more, worth of grass with a commercial mower only working 8-10 hours a day. If you are not able to do this, you do not have the right equipment for the jobs you are doing, or you have your services underpriced. I have cut over $900 worth of grass in a day by myself on several occasions.

In this case, the mowers monthly payment is covered in less than a half days' worth of work. That is a good purchase.

I always recommend buying new mowers but cannot say the same for trucks. What needs to be factored in here is called down time. Down time is when a piece of equipment is out of service because it needs to be repaired. So, you have the option of the $6k new mower or the same mower with 1,000 hours on it for $2,500. What is the better deal? I am willing to bet in the long run the new mower will have a lower cost of ownership as compared to the used mower. This is not the same for vehicles though, because they lose so much value as soon as you drive them off the lot. I recommend buying lightly used trucks that have lower miles and are still in good condition. Even after replacing three engines in my trucks over the years, I still stand by this. When you have employees, especially employees paid by the hour, the real cost of equipment failure adds up very quickly. Not only do you have the parts to pay for, but you also have the labor expense since someone is going to have to fix it. Not to mention the two or three guys on that crew who can't produce revenue for you to pay them with since the equipment just crapped out. This is why purchasing a reliable used truck is critical and why preventative maintenance is essential and should be a system within your business.

The brand of mower you buy, Exmark, or Scag, or Walker, or any other, is up to you. Whether you buy Stihl, Echo, or Redmax is going to be your personal preference, but you should put some thought into this. Can you work on the equipment? If not, you should probably buy brands that the local repair shops can fix. If you do the repairs on your equipment, is there a dealer nearby for you to quickly get parts? I would recommend buying parts online to save money, but sometimes it is worth it to pay more at the dealer and get the part now instead of waiting for them to ship to you. I started off with Exmark mowers and loved them, but when I was at the point where my business needed to purchase six new mowers, Exmark didn't make much sense anymore. I got several quotes for similar models from different manufacturers. I needed three walk behinds and three zero turns. I ended up going with Snapper Pro mowers because their quote for the six mowers was $18k less than Exmark's quote. That made it an easy decision. We have since put several hundred hours on the Snapper Pro mowers, and it was the right decision for me. Some are approaching 1,000 hours as we are wrapping up their second year of use. I honestly prefer them over Exmark now.

Regarding the equipment you use every day, it is going to be in your best interest to have backups. If you don't have the equipment available to complete the work, you will not be able to produce revenue. If you plan on growing your business, you will need to plan on re-investing most of your profit back into your business. An example would be purchasing backup equipment to allow you to continue to operate when something breaks. That brings me to another point, which is you should determine who will fix what when something breaks. If you can't work on the equipment yourself, you should already know where you are taking each piece of equipment depending on what is wrong with it. It is a bad feeling when something goes wrong and you have no plan on how to resolve it. Always keep in mind that eventually your equipment will surpass its useful life. You need to be saving money to purchase new equipment when it is necessary.

I also wanted to touch on gas versus diesel trucks. I know how cool everyone thinks diesel trucks are and I have owned two myself over the years. The fact of the matter is most companies will be just fine with gas trucks. The cost of the truck and the cost of ownership are typically less for a gas truck compared to a diesel truck. Diesel engines were designed to haul heavy loads for long distances. Hauling your trailer of mowers three to five miles at a time does not qualify. The repetitive starting and stopping of the diesel engine will quickly take its toll and end up eating away at your profit in repair costs. If you are using your trucks to haul bulk mulch, top soil, or large equipment, a diesel engine may very well be the correct purchase, but for the majority of us in this industry a gas engine will serve you better.

I would recommend finding a brand or manufacturer you like and sticking with them for your trucks and equipment. This will allow you to buy common replacement parts in bulk and have them available to fix whatever piece of equipment breaks. With the technology today the gap in quality between brands is getting narrower every day. Don't sacrifice your profit to look cool in this industry. I see it happen far too often.

Chapter 16 – Action Steps

1.– Consider buying lightly used, low mileage trucks instead of new trucks.

2.– Buy mowers new. They often have 0% or low financing terms. When everything is considered after owning the mower for several years, the cost of ownership of a new mower will be less if maintained properly as compared to purchasing a used mower 9 times out of 10.

3.– Ask your dealer if they can 'wrap' a trimmer or blower or two into your mower financing. Keep your cash in your pocket!

CHAPTER **17**

Cashing Out

We are almost to the end of the book, but we still have one significant topic to cover. I am talking about your exit strategy. If you have built a successful business, this could be a major pay day! To cash in on that major pay day, you would have had to have built a real business. No one is going to buy your job! There are also other exit strategies which include handing your business over to a family member, probably your child, or you could sell it to one of your employees. Selling it to one of your employees would more than likely entail your major pay day being spread out over the next several years as they pay you off with the profits the business generates until the purchase price is paid in full.

This is exactly where I am at in my lawn care business. I have learned so much from running it and would do it again in a heartbeat if needed. Thankfully I implemented all of the knowledge I provided in this book, and I do have a real business to sell. I will be sure to let you know how it plays out. That will definitely be a topic on our YouTube channel and on our Lawn Care Business Academy Podcast.

It is hard to determine what a business is worth. There are several different methods to evaluate a business' worth. At the end of the day, it is worth what someone is willing to pay for it. If no one is willing to buy your business, it is essentially worth nothing. I think a reasonable way to determine what the fair market value of a lawn care and landscaping business is by taking the average net profit for the past 3 years and then multiplying that number by 2 or 3. You should also add the value of your equipment to that number if you are including your equipment in the sale. You want to work with a business broker or CPA to determine the fair market value of your business. Some line items from your profit and loss and/or balance sheet should be added to or substracted from your net profit number before multiplying. Large, long term contracts could increase a business' value, or just having contracts in general, and other things like a very well built, high ranking website or lots of positive reviews can boost a business' value as well.

Chapter 17 – Action Steps

1.– Determine your exit strategy well before the time comes!

CHAPTER 18

Conclusion

Congratulations! By completing this book, you have shown the desire to increase your knowledge on how to become more profitable in your lawn and landscape business. This honestly puts you ahead of most of the other business owners out there. I have gotten to know the owners of several of the other businesses in my area, and I know they are not continuing to educate themselves on how to get better.

There was no feasible way for me to write this in a way to perfectly fit every company out there. There are also lots of other aspects of running your lawn or landscape business that will play a role in your success. That is why we have created LawnCrack.com, the Lawn Care Business Academy podcast, our LawnCrack YouTube channel, and more to come soon, to make sure we dive into every aspect of running your business and get any questions answered. We will break down different aspects of running your lawn care and landscaping business in much greater detail. I highly encourage you to check out everything we have going on. The world is changing at a rapid pace as new technology and information become available. Some things in this book may not be relevant in the future, but we keep you up to date on the latest and greatest through our other platforms.

Maybe by this point, you know why my former boss gave me the advice not to start my business. It is a lot of work, and it will be hard! There will be hiccups along your journey. Do not be afraid to fail. If you never fail, you have neglected to set your goals high enough. Failure is the best way to learn. Expect to fail and embrace it.

Before you go, I briefly wanted to touch on the subject of naysayers. Many people, even those you consider friends and family members, will say things that can cause you to lose your spirit or dreams of starting and growing your lawn care business. They may even do this unintentionally. The fact of the matter is more millionaires have been created through people starting a business than any other route possible. These people say these things because they don't understand or maybe because they are afraid to do something similar themselves. Do everything you can to surround yourself with positive people, and preferably people that are doing better than you. Don't let outside influences affect your attitude and goals. If you believe you can build a successful business, I do too.

We wish you the best in your business and would be more than happy to help in any way we can. Starting and running my business has been one of the best decisions I ever made in my life, and it can be for you too. Like the last boss I will ever have said, "There is enough grass for us all to cut." Now get out there and make it happen!

All the best,
Ryan J. Sciamanna
P.S. "Keep Making Money!"

Chapter 18 – Action Steps

1.– Start now! No matter how small of a step you take, start planning your business or start making changes to improve your business today.

2.– Never stop learning. Get your 2 free audio books from our website LawnCrack.com.

3.– Avoid naysayers. Remove negative influences from your life and/or business if you want to succeed.

4.– If you found value in this book, please leave Lawn Crack a review on Google, Yelp, and/or Facebook. We would greatly appreciate it and it will help others find our book. We want to improve the industry as a whole.

5.– Subscribe to our LawnCrack YouTube channel and to the Lawn Care Business Academy podcast which is available on iTunes, Google Play Music, and Stitcher.

AFTERWARD

I hope you are fired up and ready to create the business of your dreams. If you have not started your business yet, my hopes are this book gave you the information you needed to determine if this is a path you want to go down and has clarified a lot of the questions you have. If you have started your business, I hope this reignites your passion for your business and you do what is needed to take it to the next level.

I honestly love the versatility this industry offers. It can provide supplemental income, or you could build an empire. It is really up to you and where you want to take it. You also have lots of choices regarding the services you offer. Don't get stuck with the feeling I had when I started that I had to do it all! Experiment with offering a variety of services and determine what you are best at, what makes you the most money, and what you enjoy doing or your employees are best at performing.

Lawn Crack is here to help in any way we can, and we are not going away anytime soon! We would love for you to join our community and grow our businesses together.

Resources

Recommended Reading:
The 10X Rule by Grant Cardone
Be Obsessed or Be Average by Grant Cardone
The E-Myth Revisited by Michael E. Gerber
How to Win Friends and Influence People by Dale Carnegie
Think and Grow Rich by Napoleon Hill

Website and Internet Related:
Lawn Crack – We Built Websites that Rank and Convert Visitors into Clients
Divi – Visual Builder for WordPress
Hostgator – Affordable, Reliable Web Hosting
WordPress – More Websites are Built on the WordPress Platform than any Other Platform – You will actually install WordPress through your hosting company's site.
Zoho – Email Platform and CRM
SurveyMonkey – Survey Your Customers to Receive Valuable Feedback
Evernote – Keep Track of Everything
Wufoo – Powerful Form Builder with All Kinds of Integrations

Business Software and Tools:

Deluxe – Various Business Tools and Printing Services

QuickBooks – Accounting Software

US DOT Numbers – Requirements and General Information

SBA.gov – The Small Business Association's Official Website – Try Their Business Plan Builder Tool!

Official Trademark Website – Determine if Your Name or Slogan is Available for Use Nation Wide

IRS – The Official Internal Revenue Service's Website – Get Your EIN Here for Free

American Profit Recovery – Debt Collection Agency

DaftLogic – Area Calculator to Measure Square Footage

NOLO – Legal Advice and Tools

Health:

BodyBuilding.com – Supplements for Workouts

Plug and Play Profit and Loss Statement – Resource Created by Lawn Crack

While You Work:

Amazon Unlimited Music Free Trial - Music

Audible Free Trial – Audio Books

Lawn Crack:

Lawn Crack – Tools, Resources, and Information to Build a Profitable Lawn and Landscape Company

Lawn Crack on YouTube

Lawn Crack on Instagram

Lawn Crack on Facebook

Lawn Crack's Facebook Group

Lawn Care Business Academy – Lawn Crack's Official Podcast

Business and Life Coaching:

Maximizing Results – Helping People Maximize Their Potential in Life

Profit Solutions Group – Business Coaching and Consulting

Green Industry Publications:
Turf Magazine
Lawn and Landscape

Design and Printing Needs:
Fiverr – Great Place for Cheap Professional Design Work

Banking:
Chase Bank – Nationwide Bank with Lots of Incentives for Small Businesses, Business Credit Card, and Payment Processing

Conferences and Tradeshows:
GIE+Expo – Largest Green Industry Trade Show in the World!
Service Autopilot Conference (SA5 will be 2018's, SA6 will be 2019's, and so on. There is not a dedicated website for this conference yet.)

New and Used Trucks, Equipment, Parts, and Supplies for Sale:
Uhaul
Craigslist
Amazon
eBay
Home Depot Tool Rental Sales
Lawn Crack
Gregson Clark – Eco-505 Spray Tank Addition

Marketing and Advertising Related:
5DollarSigns – Cheap 'Yard Signs' for Advertising
Google – Verify Your Website with Google
Bing – Verify Your Website with Bing
EDDM by USPS – Targeting Marketing by the United States Postal Service
Radius Bomb – Hyper Targeted Postal Mail Marketing
Angie's List
Thumbtack
Home Advisor

Find Employees:
ZipRecruiter
Indeed
Craigslist

Routing, Scheduling, and Invoicing Software:
Service Autopilot – This is the Only One we can Recommend

Made in the USA
San Bernardino, CA
28 December 2018